Nkrumah and Ghana

'Kwame Nkrumah was the man that salted Africa.'

Nkrumah and Ghana:

The Dilemma of Post-Colonial Power

Kofi Buenor Hadjor

Kegan Paul International
London and New York

First published in 1988 by Kegan Paul
International Limited, 11 New Fetter Lane,
London EC4P 4EE

Distributed by
Associated Book Publishers (UK) Ltd
11 New Fetter Lane, London EC4P 4EE

Routledge, Chapman & Hall Inc.
29 West 35th Street
New York, NY 10001, USA

Produced by Worts-Power Associates

Set in Times
by Papyrus Printers & Stationers Ltd
Thetford, Norfolk
and printed in Great Britain
by Dotesios Printers, Ltd
Bradford-on-Avon, Wiltshire.

ISBN 0 7103 0322 X

Contents

Dedication

For the people of Ghana
and for Philip Yossifov Hadjor and
his mother, Sheshinka Avramova, and
for the memory of Dr Emmanuel Hansen who died tragically
in Arusha, Tanzania, on Friday, 13 November 1987

Preface and Acknowledgements

This book has been a long time in coming. During the days following Kwame Nkrumah's death in 1972, the idea of writing this book first took form. While thinking about what form the book ought to take, I remembered his advice to us in Conakry – 'learn that you can carry on the fight'. Back in 1972, I still had a lot of learning to do. With hindsight, it is as well that this project was postponed.

During the past fifteen years, Africa has gone through a major trauma. The events of these years help throw light on the Nkrumah experiment, and underline its continued relevance for Ghana and for Africa. The test of time has proved in Nkrumah's favour. It has provided the author with material evidence of the continuity of the issues which Nkrumah sought to address. The recent revival of interest in Nkrumah throughout Africa, and Ghana in particular, confirms that this book was not written in a vacuum. Ghana and Africa must still do a lot of learning and struggling. We hope this work will convince our readers that it is so, and take on board the best of the tradition that we inherited from Nkrumah. And in line with Nkrumah's emphasis on making knowledge accessible to the widest possible audience, we have also written a popular version of this text[1], particularly aimed at Africa's youth.

Many friends and colleagues have given me tremendous support in the writing of this book. Special thanks, however, go to the following:
- Patrick Smith, Dede-Esi Amanor and Judy Hirst for researching most of the text,
- Pauline Tiffen for the index,
- Cary Yageman for inputting the entire manuscript into the computer,

1 Kwame Nkrumah, *A Beginners' Guide to African Liberation.* London and Accra, Third World Communications, 1988.

— Kabral Blay-Amihere for providing the bibliography,
— Sharmini Brookes, Laura and Ruth Brako also deserve my thanks for their various roles,
— my thoughts for Kemi and Joy.

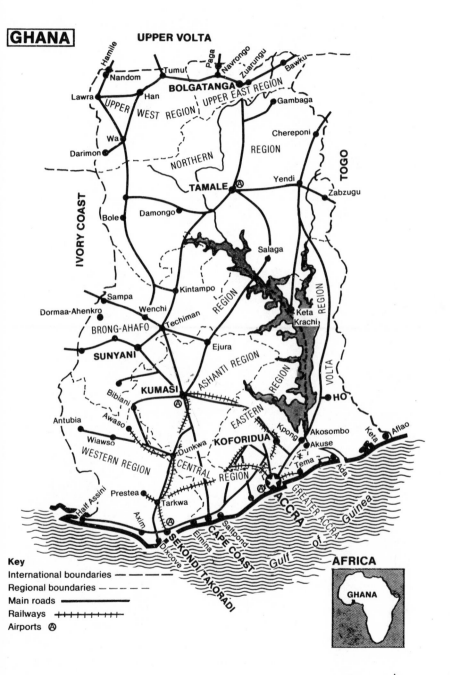

ix

Introduction

by
John K. Tettegah[1]

Kwame Nkrumah died in April 1972, more than fifteen years ago. For those of us who knew him it appears as if the great tribune is still with us today. His powerful message and analysis of the African condition are confirmed every month, year after year.

Throughout his life, Nkrumah was in the forefront of the struggle to build a new Africa. His pioneering efforts in the field of anti-colonial resistance, political analysis and philosophy are now recognised throughout the world. He was above all a natural leader of his people. To a considerable extent it was his leadership that was responsible for ensuring that Ghana would become the first African nation to win its political independence in the post-war period. Under Nkrumah Ghana became the centre of the African revolution, setting the pace for the rest of the continent.

Those who opposed change in Africa looked upon Nkrumah as their most bitter enemy. In the Western media he was constantly vilified as a dangerous trouble-maker. On many occasions he was the target of assassination attempts. In the end the CIA organised an attempt to overthrow his government in 1966. The enemies of Africa were determined to destroy him. While they succeeded in forcing him into exile, they failed to discredit the man. Nkrumah would not be silenced. To his last day Nkrumah breathed the fire of

1 John K. Tettegah is now Ghana's Ambassador in Moscow. His leader-ship of the Ghana Trades Union Congress and the All-African Trades Union Federation (AATUF) made him a well-known political personality in the sixties. Both he and the author shared Nkrumah's exile years.

1

African freedom and unity. Africa still has much to learn from Nkrumah. No African nation can feel safe in an international order where foreign adventurers are free to prey on the continent. The world economic order is a hostile force which continues to plunder Africa's resources. Unequal terms of trade and exorbitant interest rates ensure that every year a significant portion of Africa's wealth is lost to the continent. A network of foreign military forces – American, British, French – spread all over the continent stand prepared to back up those economic interests. The apartheid regime of Pretoria is a permanent threat too. The threat of war and foreign intervention hangs over much of Africa indicating that the struggle against colonialism has not yet been won.

All this Nkrumah anticipates in his writings. Nkrumah knew that even political independence was only a temporary gain. The former colonial powers were not prepared to abandon their stake in Africa. By hook or crook they have sought to keep Africa under their control. Nkrumah would not have been surprised at the invasion of Angola and Mozambique or the air raid on Libya. He argued convincingly that if Africa could not be united it would be destroyed.

And yet Nkrumah was essentially an optimist. He had profound faith in the energy and dynamism of Africa. He knew that history is on Africa's side. His main concern was to ensure that his people were ready to assume the responsibility thrown on them by history. For the new generation of Africans Nkrumah represents the essential starting-point. *Nkrumah and Ghana* reconstructs Nkrumah's life so that the reader can share in his rich experience.

It was only a question of time before Hadjor's authoritative analysis of Kwame Nkrumah's life would appear. During our exile in Conakry and Cairo, Hadjor and I were both concerned that the lessons of Nkrumah's experience should not be lost to the future generations of Ghana in particular and the rest of Africa in general. It was at this point in time that the ideas contained in the work began to take shape.

As a young journalist working for Nkrumah, and yet not part of the inner circle, Hadjor was well placed to initiate this work. First-hand acquaintance with Nkrumah, as well as distance, has helped Hadjor to write a book which combines a firm commitment to the objectives of Nkrumah with a remarkably balanced assessment of this critical chapter in Ghana's history.

Nkrumah did not suffer fools. He was impatient because he wanted his people to realise a liberation that was long overdue. He did not let his impatience get the better of him. He was always concerned to clarify and understand. One hopes that his sense of urgency tempered by an acute sense of insight has been conveyed to the reader in this book. Nkrumah does not need admirers. Were he alive today he would say: 'Take up my sword, fight our own battles and learn, learn and learn, so that Africa can assume its rightful place in the history of humanity.'

Hadjor's *Nkrumah and Ghana*, in my opinion, is the last verdict on the great Osagyefo, and deserves to be widely read throughout Africa and by non-Africans studying African history and politics.

Chapter 1

Ghana in History

In the very early days of the Christian era, long before
England had assumed any importance, long before even her
people had united into a nation, our ancestors had attained a
great empire which lasted until the eleventh century, when it
fell before the attacks of the Moors of the North. At its
height that empire stretched from Timbuktu to Bamako and
even as far as the Atlantic. It is said that lawyers and scholars
were much respected in that empire and that the inhabitants
of Ghana wore garments of wool, cotton, silk and velvet.
There was trade in copper, gold and textile fabrics and jewels
and weapons of gold and silver were carried.[1]

Kwame Nkrumah, like other Pan-Africanists before him (W. E. B.
DuBois, George Padmore and Sylvester Williams), was determined
to rescue Africa's glorious history from colonialism. Across the
continent the European colonisers had sought to deny Africa a
history, partly because of their own ignorance and laziness and
partly as a means to justify the atrocities of colonialism. After all, if
you are dealing with ignorant savages without a history of their
own, the colonisers reasoned, how can it be a crime to come and
take over their society and get what you can in the process?
Nkrumah wanted to nail that lie right away. Of course, Africa and
Africans had a history – in fact, it is a history that goes back further
than that of the so-called civilised peoples of Europe. Indeed,

1 Kwame Nkrumah, *Autobiography of Kwame Nkrumah*, London,
Heinemann, 1957, p. 163.

4

Africa is today regarded by most archaeologists and anthropologists as the cradle of humankind, and it is thought that the first
Homo sapiens originated from the area now known as Kenya
several million years ago.

Africans can cite many texts in support of their arguments – a
Spanish Arab called Al-Bakri wrote extensively about the Ghana
empire as a highly organised society in 1067. This was just one year
after the Angles and Saxons in Britain had been invaded by William
the Conqueror. There are successive accounts given by European
traders of the conditions in West Africa in the fourteenth and
fifteenth centuries which indicate a high level of organisation and
planning. For example, a Dutch traveller visiting the city of Benin
described it thus:

> When you go into it you enter a great broad street, which is
> not paved and seems to be seven or eight times broader than
> the Warmoes Street in Amsterdam. This street is straight and
> does not bend at any point. It is thought to be four miles long.
> The houses in this town stand in good order one close and
> evenly placed with its neighbour, just as the houses in
> Holland stand. They have square rooms, sheltered by a roof
> that is open in the middle, where the rain, wind and light
> come in. The King's yard is very great. It is built around
> many square-shaped yards. These yards have surrounding
> galleries where sentries are placed.[2]

And down in southern Africa are the remnants of a settlement
called Great Zimbabwe. The buildings which comprise Great
Zimbabwe were of such a degree of sophistication that Cecil
Rhodes and his band of colonisers – misled by their own racism and
wishful thinking – said that the settlement must have been constructed by earlier European visitors. And it was only in the second
half of this century that there was enough evidence to prove that the
stone settlement had been built by Africans. So history is not just
another subject to be taught to schoolchildren, or an interesting
series of stories; it affects the way in which we see ourselves and our
capabilities. That is why Nkrumah and his colleagues used to say:
'Know your history to help share your future!'

2 Basil Davidson, *Discovering Africa's Past*, pp. 122–3.

Nkrumah and his colleagues in the independence movement insisted that the name 'Gold Coast' – the colonial name for Ghana – should not be used. What's in a name? you might ask. The answer is that by calling our country 'Gold Coast' the colonisers were saying their prime interest in the land was the valuable minerals in our territory, and not the people and their development. Otherwise, why did they not call Britain 'Island of Coal'? Of course they did not because such a name would be derogatory to the people and their culture. Accordingly, one of the strongest demands of Nkrumah and the independence movement was to change the colonisers' name of 'Gold Coast' to 'Ghana' as a tribute to the history of our various peoples. Again in his *Motion of Destiny* speech, Nkrumah told the Legislative Assembly in Accra:

> We take pride in the name of Ghana, not out of romanticism, but as an inspiration for the future. It is right and proper that we should know about our past. For just as the future emerges from the present, so has the present emerged from the past. Nor need we be ashamed of our past. There was much in it of glory. What our ancestors achieved in the context of their contemporary society gives us confidence that we can create, out of the past, a glorious future, not in terms of war and military pomp, but in terms of social progress and peace.[3]

History too, Nkrumah pointed out, teaches us what others have achieved before us and how we can build on the best of these traditions:

> As with our enslaved brothers dragged from these shores to the United States and to the West Indies, throughout our tortuous history we have not been docile under the heel of the conqueror. Having known by our own traditions and experienced the essentiality of unity and of government, we constantly formed ourselves into cohesive blocks as a means of resistance against the alien force within our borders.[4]

3 Nkrumah, *Autobiography*, p. 163.
4 Ibid., pp. 163–4

Ghana at the Beginning

The earliest written records that refer to Ghana date back to about AD 770, when it was described as the 'land of gold' by an Arab traveller called Al-Fazari. But Ghana was originally the name given to the state of Wagadu, which was one of the biggest in ancient West Africa. We must go back even further to see how West Africa developed as a distinct region from North and East Africa. For since that time, West Africa has always been in a unique position: because of its isolation it has been able to preserve much of its culture and tradition, but at the same time it has been cut off from some of the more important intellectual and technological developments in the rest of the world.

West Africa's isolation was brought about by the gradual encroachment of the Sahara Desert. Around 2000 BC – that is, about a thousand years after the people of West Africa had started organising agriculture and farm settlements – the rivers of the Sahara began to fail, and, gradually, its farming people moved away, dispersing to West, North and East Africa. This migration was completed around 500 BC when most of the discoveries of the New Stone Age had been taken into the West African region, though there is growing, but not yet conclusive evidence that the early West Africans had developed their own forms of agriculture, developing unique strains of rice.

Because of the lack of written records about West Africa at this time, we are dependent on archaeological evidence for these developments, and on our own oral history which has been passed down from generation to generation. For example, the Akan and Nzima say their ancestors came from far in the north, perhaps during the great migration in the face of the spreading Sahara, while the Ga and Ewe peoples say their ancestors came from the east.

Of course, these legends and traditions refer to a small group who set out from the previous homeland to find new areas of habitation where they would meet other traditions. These migrations – this mixing of old and new cultures – is what makes up history, but it is important to understand that in the West African context most of the migrations after 500 BC were confined to within the West Africa region. So nearly all the inhabitants of West Africa today are descendants of people who have lived in this region for over 1,500 years.

Iron and Trade

The development of organised agriculture increased the supplies of food which in turn increased the size of the populations, as well as allowing these societies to support persons who neither grew nor gathered food. These peoples were then free to develop primitive technology, like the making of simple tools. The ancient Africans (in what is now called Egypt) were making tools with copper and gold more than five thousand years ago, but these metals were unsatisfactory – both because they were too scarce and therefore valuable in themselves and because they were too soft to make durable tools.

It was the Asian people called the Hittites who discovered in 1500 BC how to make iron, a metal out of which hard tools and weapons could be forged. These techniques reached the Nile Valley and the ancient Ethiopians by about 600 BC, and took another three hundred years to get to the West Africans. The archaeological evidence is that West Africa's first iron smelters lived by the banks of the Benue and Niger rivers, but quickly spread their knowledge in the region. Iron meant better tools and better weapons. Iron enabled travellers to clear a way through the forest to reach other areas and hunters to capture and kill wild animals. And iron also brought a new source of military power. Those who had the better iron weapons were able to conquer and rule their neighbours, and, as the groups came into conflict, the stronger ones would predominate and set up simple forms of government to control the people they had conquered. As the societies grew more complex, labour was divided between the farmers, the hunters, the tool-makers, the warriors and the traders, and to hold all this together they needed some forms of basic political organisation.

With these technological developments people expanded trade with each other – exchanging produce and tools, as they exchanged knowledge and cultures. The early history was entirely a history of battle after battle. The development of the early states was then subject to the level of technology that had developed, the organisa-tion of their labour force, their geographical locations, the natural resources available to them, and their trading relationships with the outside world.

As a general rule, those states situated on the main trade routes tended to be more centrally controlled, needing as they did to make firm decisions about the sale and purchase of products, whereas those groups who lived away from the main centres of trade tended to develop looser, less centralised systems of government.

Ancient Ghana

Early records place the origins of the Ghanaian empire at about AD 300. The state grew out of its peoples' need to protect their trade and its heart lay in the market centres around the upper waters of the Niger and the Senegal rivers. These markets stood where trading routes which came northward from the gold-producing areas of West Africa met trading caravan routes which crossed the Sahara from North Africa. So the traders in these market centres developed by buying gold and ivory from the traders of West Africa and selling these goods to the traders of North Africa in exchange for Saharan salt and other North African produce. This strategic position also meant that they needed a strong system of government to defend their markets and play some role in the control of the respective trade routes.

The evidence is that it was the Soninke people who founded ancient Ghana – a state which, through commercial influence and military power, developed into an empire controlling a large region all around it (see map). Again the evidence from the written records found in Timbuktu is that the first Ghanaian king was crowned around AD 300. Not much is known about how the line of the Soninke kings started, but it is presumed that the merchants decided to choose a king from one of their number as a means of regulating their trade, as well as having religious and other cultural leadership functions.

The Spanish Arab traveller Al-Bakri, who collected together several accounts of the Ghanaian empire, describes how the expansion of the kingdom's trade increased the wealth of the kingdom so that the king could control all the smaller kingdoms in the surrounding areas, employ hundreds of messengers and other servants and develop the means to organise such an empire. Piecing together accounts from Muslim travellers of the day, Al-Bakri described the

9

court of the Ghanaian emperor, King Tunka Manin, in about AD 1065 thus:

> When the king gives audience to his people, to listen to their complaints and to set them to rights, he sits in a pavilion around which stand ten pages holding shields and gold mounted swords. On his right hand are the sons of princes of his empire, splendidly clad with gold plaited into their hair. The governor of the city is seated on the ground in front of the king and all around him are his counsellors in the same position. The gates of the chamber are guarded by dogs of an excellent breed. These dogs never leave their place of duty. They wear collars of gold and silver, ornamented with metals. The beginning of a royal meeting is announced by the beating of a kind of drum they call *deba*. The drum is made of a long piece of hollowed wood. The people gather when they hear its sound.[5]

Other later accounts substantiate these descriptions of the sumptuous Ghanaian court. A writer in Timbuktu called Mahud Kati describes how a Ghanaian king called Kanissa'ai possessed a thousand horses and how 'each of these horses slept only on a carpet with a silken rope for halter', and would have three personal attendants and was generally looked after like royalty itself. Other stories – doubtless embroidered with the passage of time – tell how the Ghanaian kings would hold banquets for ten thousand people at a time and dispense gifts to all comers.

We do know from available archaeological evidence that Ghana's last capital at Kumbi Saleh – about 320 miles north of modern Bamako – was the biggest West African city of its day, with a population of over fifteen thousand. And again, according to Al-Bakri, the ancient Ghanaian kings were masters of a large empire and a formidable power: they could put two hundred thousand warriors into the field, with more than forty thousand of them armed with bows and arrows.

5 Davidson, *Discovering Africa's Past*, p. 69.

Governing Ghana's empire

Ghana's position as middleman at the crossroads of trade between the gold and ivory producers of the south and the Berber traders of the north was a great commercial strength, but it also meant that the kingdom would have to develop defences against attack.

The state had the means to protect itself. It had a large population and it had the iron-making technology to produce effective weapons, so the Ghanaian rulers developed a type of security zone around their state. They strengthened their position as middleman by bringing lesser states like Takur under their control and pushed southwards to where the gold and ivory were coming from.

They also pushed northwards and took over southern Saharan cities like Audoghast. As the empire and the trading network expanded, so the system of government grew more sophisticated. A Ghanaian king then appointed lesser kings as governors to look after his interests in distant provinces in return for specified remunerations. The number of a Ghanaian king's subjects grew as more and more people gave their loyalty – and paid their taxes – to the central government.

Ghana's Riches

Both the resplendent appearance of the court and the fact that a king could put so many men under arms indicate that he must have been fabulously wealthy. He obtained his money primarily through taxes: he levied a tax on goods coming into the state and another, higher tax on all goods going out. These taxes applied to all goods of value like gold, salt and copper.

Apart from this a Ghanaian king decreed that all gold found in the state belonged to him, which was both a means of building up the royal wealth and of controlling the sale of gold so as to keep its price high. Just like today's mineral monopolies which seek to control the price of diamonds, gold and platinum, the ancient Ghanaian kings used their power of monopoly to protect their incomes. In this, Ghana's trading position was crucial. About the time of the rise of Ghana, the gold mines of Europe and western Asia were being exhausted. Thus began the history of European trade with West Africa – a trade primarily in search of gold. Ghana really began the trade in gold and, as time went by, other peoples began to copy Ghana's success.

The Fall of the Ghanaian empire

As it was, the Ghanaian empire was not invincible, and various warring groups started making incursions into the empire in search of some of the obviously rich pickings. Chief among these groups were the Berber warriors from the Mauritanian Sahara in the north-west who wanted to leave their impoverished environment for richer pastures. So they migrated south under the tutelage of a religious leader called Abdullah ibn Yasin. He established a centre of Muslim teaching called the Hermitage. Those who attended the centre were called the peoples of the Hermitage, Al Murbethin or the Almoravids. The Almoravids quickly gathered their forces and travelled to convert the rulers of those states in far western Africa and the Berber communities under their control. This gave the Almoravids the strength to move northwards attacking Morocco, crossing the Straits of Gibraltar and then taking over Al Andalus and Muslim Spain. At the same time a southern wing of the Almoravid movement moved against Ghana. Its leader, Abu Bakr, leading a Berber confederation, joined forces with the people of Takur to wage a long war against the Ghanaian empire. Abu Bakr's army took the city of Audoghast in 1054.

Under the weight of these attacks, the Ghanaian empire began to fall apart, but the early Ghanaians showed an admirable spirit of resistance. There was a succession of revolts against the new rulers, and Abu Bakr was killed while trying to suppress a Ghanaian resistance movement in 1087.

As the Ghanaian empire fell apart, other groups like the Fulani who lived side by side with the Soninke (the founders of Ghana) rose up. The Fulani rose in Tukur, the northern part of modern Senegal, and by about 1203 they had taken control of the kingdom of Diara, a former province of Kaniaga, another old Ghanaian province. However, these new would-be rulers of ancient Ghana did not meet with much success. The Muslim traders of Kumbi rejected Sumanguru's rule for religious and commercial reasons and moved northwards to found a new city. Then the Mandika people from Kangaba challenged Sumanguru to a battle in which he was defeated and killed.

The Rise of Mali: the Ghanaians Migrate

Taking over where the Ghanaian empire left off, the Mali empire rose to even greater heights and remained a powerful empire between 1200 and 1400, when it was finally split asunder by the dissension of its subject peoples. In the meantime the ancestors of modern Ghanaians – particularly the Akan peoples – began their migration southwards towards their present homeland. Historians say the ancient Ghanaians migrated partly to escape the chaos and confusion that followed the demise of old Ghana and also to escape subjection under the Malian empire.

By about 1200, the Akan were already beginning to settle in what is now called northern Asante, as did other groups like the founders of Denkyira, Adansi, Fante, Adwamu and others. The new Ghana that was forming took on small units of social organisation as the new habitat was dense forest, which inhibited the good communications necessary to run a powerful, centralised state.

Of the states founded in this era, the best known is Bono in the Takyiman area. It was through Bono that the principal trade with the states and empires of the Western Sudan became important. Traditional folk history states that a strong chief called Asaman and his queen mother, Amayaa, founded Bono. The traditions of early Bono have it that gold was discovered in the Twi River and around Perembomase, but it is more likely that the gold was discovered many years previously and that it was only really exploited in Asaman's reign. What is certain is that the increasing gold output from Bono coincided with a general rise in demand for gold from the Western Sudan and so helped influence the political and economic developments of the region.

This upsurge in the demand for gold from Bono happened

13

around 1400, about the same time as the foundation of the early states of the Fante and other Akan peoples, as well as non-Akan peoples like the Nzima (Nkrumah's people) to their west and the Ga-Adangme and Ewe to their east. It was these people in small communities dotted along what was then called the Guinea coast who first met Portuguese traders in the fifteenth century.

Soon after their arrival on the coast, the Portuguese asked for permission to build a castle in the Elmina district. They undertook negotiations in 1482 with Kwamina Ansah at Elmina, as a contemporary diarist recorded:

> Kwamina Ansah was seated on a high chair dressed in a jacket of brocade with a chair of precious stones and his chiefs were all dressed in silk . . . these noblemen wore rings and golden jewels on their heads and beards. The King came in their midst, his legs and arms covered with golden bracelets and rings, a collar around his neck, from which hung small bells, and in his plaited beard golden bars, which weighed down its untrimmed hair, so that instead of being twisted it was smooth. To show his dignity, he walked with very slow and light steps, never turning his head to either side.[6]

The Portuguese account goes on to describe Kwamina Ansah as a man of good understanding 'both by nature and by his dealings with the crews of the trading ships and he possessed a clear judgement. And as one who not only listened to the translation of the interpreter, but who watched each gesture made by Diego de Azambuja; and while this continued, both he and his men were completely silent; no one so much as spat, so perfectly disciplined were they.'

This and similar accounts tell us that these coastal states developing in the fifteenth and sixteenth centuries were small but firmly controlled, with chiefs, counsellors, organised governments, tightly regulated codes of public behaviour and a willingness to organise trade links both with sea voyagers from Europe and with the peoples of the interior.

It was on this basis of trade that the various states that make up modern Ghana developed – that is, the coastal states and their

6 Ibid.

trade with the European seafarers and the inland states which were developing gold production and accordingly stepping up their trade with Western Sudan. For many years the trade with the north remained more valuable than the trade on the coast, but, by the mid-sixteenth century, the British, the Danes and the Swedes had joined the Portuguese in the queue of European seafarers wanting to do business with the coastal states.

It was around this time that the trade in enslaved human beings started. The Atlantic slave trade grew quickly from a small base to service the Europeans' attempts to colonise another continent – this time what we now call the Americas. If anything, the European colonisation of the Americas was even more brutal than that of Africa: rather than try to make deals with the indigenous Indians of America, the Europeans attempted to wipe them out. One Spanish report of 1518 said that only twenty-six years after the first voyage of Columbus across the Atlantic, the Spanish traders had managed to wipe out more than a million of the indigenous inhabitants of the island we now call Cuba. The surviving Indians were sent to work in the mines or on the plantations of the newly colonised Americas.

As the wealth and size of the American plantation colonies grew, so did the demand for slave labour. And accordingly, the merchants developed a system which became known as 'triangular trade'. Triangular trade was so called because it had three distinct sides or stages, each of which brought profit to the merchants and factory owners of Western Europe. In the first side of the triangle, the European merchants bought and shipped to West Africa goods such as cotton, alcoholic spirits, metal ware and firearms. These goods were bartered in exchange for slaves. The Africans sold were already slaves in the sense that they were prisoners or condemned criminals, but if they had stayed on in West Africa they would have been treated as household or domestic slaves, a fate far less harsh than the terrible one suffered on their forced journey across the Atlantic.

The second side of the triangle was the journey taking these slaves across the Atlantic to the Americas, where they were sold to the plantation owners for sugar and tobacco and other exotic products. The third and final side of the triangle was the shipping of the American products back to Europe and their sale for very high prices. Other Europeans soon saw the immense profits to be made in this appalling trade in human beings, to the extent that they stopped buying gold and other minerals in favour of enslaved Africans.

As the eminent historian Basil Davidson writes: 'This slave trade greatly enriched Britain and France as well as other Western Europeans. But it made Africa poorer. The beginnings of this evil trade were part of the sixteenth century. The cloud then was no bigger than a man's hand, but soon it grew into a tempest and the tempest of the slave trade blew and raged for years, even for centuries.'[7]

And so began one of the most tragic chapters in human history; it was a chapter that would lead, as surely as day follows night, to one of the greatest liberation movements in the history of the world, a liberation movement described vividly by Nkrumah in his seminal work on Pan-Africanism, *Africa Must Unite*: 'The great millions of Africa and of Asia, have grown impatient of being hewers of wood and drawers of water, and are rebelling against the false belief that providence created some to be the menials of others.'[8] What stands out in Nkrumah's analysis of this tragic but eventually joyous liberating history is his belief that the goodness and greatness of the human spirit can and will conquer the evil that men do. As he describes how the ravages of the slave trade led to colonialism, Nkrumah urges the reader to analyse and learn, rather than merely recriminate as he said elsewhere

> It was not that a nasty minded bunch of men awoke simultaneously one morning in England, France, Belgium, Germany and Portugal or in any of the other colonial countries and decided that it would be a good thing to jump into Africa and grind the peoples' noses into the dust so that they could all of them retire to their homeland in due course, rich and happy from Africa's hardship. It was a good deal more complex than that, despite the plundering compulsions that sent the Portuguese and others out as early as the fifteenth century to pluck Africa's gold and ivory, and later its human treasure, to enrich the coffers of Western monarchs and merchants.

7 Ibid.
8 Ibid.

Chapter 2

The British Move In

The slave traders prospered until the early nineteenth century and laid down the foundation for the colonial linkage of African societies and economies to the increasingly powerful states in Western Europe. It was a period of great change and competition among the warring European states, which vied with one another for the right to exploit the spoils of Africa. At the same time the peoples of West Africa also fought among themselves, but ultimately united to fight the common enemy of colonialism. In this sense, the despicable triangular trade of the slave merchants sowed the seeds of its own destruction: the slave trade eventually created a common bond among those Africans still in the motherland and those shipped over to the Americas and the West Indies and those in Europe. This was the basis of the Pan-African movement which has proved so crucial in shaping the destiny of Africa. Of course, from the outset there was African opposition to the slave trade, and that is why the European slave merchants preferred to deal with those local chieftains and monarchs who were prepared to enter into the trade on a peaceable basis. But it was from the sporadic African opposition to the slave trade that the wider Pan-African movement grew – the movement with a crucial influence in Kwame Nkrumah's intellectual development.

What is important to realize is that the slave-trade system was not destroyed simply through the good offices of a few European philanthropists. Rather, it was the combination of Africa-based political opposition, joined with the liberalism in European thought engendered by the French and American revolutions, and, ultimately, the pursuit of economic self-interest by the colonising powers, which gradually made the slave trade irrelevant to their strategies. It should not be forgotten that many prominent Europeans in the anti-slavery movement proceeded to use the fruits of colonialism to run factories where they more or less enslaved their own people in the most hideous working conditions for derisory wages.

In his book *Towards Colonial Freedom*, written in 1947, Nkrumah defines this crucial relationship between colonialism and the industrial development of Europe and the Africans' continuing attempt to break the chains that bound them. Nkrumah argued that socialist thinkers like Marx and Lenin had truly understood the workings of colonialism and its legacy. The Marxist–Leninist analysis is that the essence of colonialism is the exploitation of the colonies for their sources of raw materials and the setting up of an exclusive economic relationship between the colonising country and the colony, and, of course, the willingness to defend that relationship through force of arms if necessary. Summarising all this, Nkrumah wrote in *Towards Colonial Freedom*:

> The colonies are thus a source of raw materials and cheap labour, a dumping ground for spurious surplus goods to be sold at exorbitant prices. Therefore these colonies become avenues for capital investment, not for the benefit and development of the colonial peoples, but for the benefit of the investors, whose agents are the governments concerned.[1]

But Nkrumah was quick to point out, as Marx and Lenin had done before him, that this system created the conditions for its own destruction by helping 'the emergence of a colonial intelligentsia' which in turn awakens 'national consciousness among colonial peoples'.[2]

This awakening of national consciousness was, of course, a long and uneven process – in part, the colonial relationships in Africa were ambivalent and complex. The African establishment, as it was then constituted by the monarchs and chieftains, was very willing to do business with the European traders who were essentially the

1 Kwame Nkrumah, *Towards Colonial Freedom*, London, Panaf, 1973, pp. xvii.
2 Ibid.

forerunners of colonialism. This was particularly so in Ghana, where the European traders built more trading castles along the coastline than in any other Western African state.

The Europeans built forty-one trading castles in Ghana. For many years, while the Europeans remained masters at sea, the Ghanaians controlled the land. The Ghanaians defined the terms of trade and the conditions for setting up trading establishments. At first it was easier for them to do this as the Europeans were so divided among themselves – all of them trying to compete for influence and access to Ghana's rich minerals. The Ghanaians were able to exploit these divisions by changing their alliances with the European traders and playing them off against each other.

A Dutch official at Elmina Castle, William Bosman, wrote home to a friend in 1700 that Ghanaians had skilfully protected the access to their gold to ensure that they controlled the terms of the trade:

> There is no small number of men in Europe who believe that the gold mines are in our power, and that we, like the Spanish in the West Indies, have nothing more to do than to work the mines with our slaves. But you should understand that we have no means of getting to these treasures, nor do I believe that any of our people have ever seen a single one of these mines.[3]

The great trading castles built along Ghana's coastline – like Elmina, Akim, Cape Coast, Cormantin, Christiansborg and Anomabu – were not the symbols of European power that some have taken them to be. The Europeans had to pay rent for the castles, and they had only very limited power to guard the castles and control the nearby land. During disputes, they were attacked in their castles by African armies. In one case in 1693, Akwamu's soldiers seized the big Danish fort of Christiansborg in Accra from the Danes. In order to regain control the Danes were compelled to pay a large ransom of gold.

About this time in the early eighteenth century there were important changes in the nature of military power. With the increasing use of firearms the European armies became more

3 Ibid.

professionalised; that is, their soldiers would be paid for their services, rather than merely being reluctant conscripts in a colonial adventure. At the height of eighteenth-century trade with West Africa the gunsmiths of the English Midlands were producing more than a hundred thousand guns a year for West Africa. The African armies demanded guns as part of their trade with the Europeans, but they proved to be double-edged weapons. The guns strengthened the Africans' ability to defend themselves against attack, but at the same time they promoted much of the internecine strife that served to weaken African unity. However, the Africans' mastery of firearms techniques clearly impressed the European traders. Again the Dutch trader William Bosman mentions this in a letter home to Holland at the beginning of the eighteenth century:

> The main weapons of [the Ghanaian Africans] are muskets and carbines, in the use of which these Africans are wonderfully skilled. It is a real pleasure to watch them train their armies. They handle their weapons so cleverly, shooting them off in several ways, one man sitting, another creeping along the ground or lying down, that it is surprising that they do not hurt each other. Perhaps you will wonder how the Africans came to be furnished with these firearms. But you should know that we sell them very great quantities, and doing this we offer them a knife with which to cut their own throats. But we are forced to do this. For if we, the Dutch, did not do this, they would easily get enough muskets from the English or from the Danes or the Prussians. And even if we governors of the official European trading corporations could all agree to stop selling firearms, the private traders of the English or the Dutch would go on selling them.[4]

In the pattern of shifting alliances that evolved in West Africa during this period from the beginning of the eighteenth century until the end of the nineteenth century, the Europeans gradually worked out a more rational division of their military and commercial objectives while the Africans continued for some time to fight their battles on two flanks – against each other and against the growing European intrusion into their land.

4 B. Davidson, *Discovering Africa's Past*, p. 129.

Although by 1400 several strong Akan states had developed – the Fante, Akim and Denkyira – it was the Asante which became the most important and the most troublesome for the European invaders. Earlier, the Asante people had been unable to exploit fully the advantages of their access to Ghana's gold: they were disunited and had fallen under the overlordship of other, much stronger Akan groups. But by the middle of the seventeenth century the Asante resistance grew stronger, and in 1695 their leader, Osei Tutu, together with a priest of the Asante religion called Akufo Anokye, established a strong hold over their people with a joint political and spiritual leadership. Anokye told the Asante people that their god, Nyame, had decreed that they should be united under one strong leader for the betterment of their peoples. The symbol of this unity was to be a sacred golden stool, which it would be the duty of every king to guard and respect, but no king or commoner would ever be allowed to sit on it.

In less than ten years the Asante Union achieved its results. The Asante people won their independence from their neighbours and secured a direct channel of trade with the Europeans on the coast. Two notable warrior kings – Opoku Ware and Osei Kojo – continued the work of Osei Tutu by consolidating the Asante's military gains and building up an efficient civil service. The new system of government evolved in part to protect the new areas under Asante control, and in part to administer the increasingly important long-distance trade with the Sudanese in the east and with the Europeans on the coast.

In the process, Kumasi, the seat of government, became a bustling cosmopolitan city. The Asante had no objection to employing foreigners if they had useful skills to teach: Scots, French and Germans were employed in trading administration and military training, while West Africans like the Muslim scholars from the Sudan and the Hausa traders from what is now called Nigeria worked in harmony with the Asante in Kumasi.

In 1817 an Englishman called Thomas Bowdich, who was sent to negotiate a trading and political agreement with King Osei Bonsu, was clearly impressed with the administration of Kumasi. In his diary he notes that he had been received by the King with manners that were 'majestic yet courteous' and found the Asante capital to be a colourful and clean town:

21

Four of the main streets are half a mile long, and between
fifty and a hundred yards wide. Each is in the charge of a
senior captain. Each household has to burn its rubbish every
morning at the back of the street. The people are as clean
and careful about the appearance of their houses as they are
about themselves.[5]

At the time Bowdich was writing, the Asante empire extended over
an area which comprises more or less the whole of what is now
known as modern Ghana, as well as parts of what are now known as
Côte d'Ivoire and Togo. By 1807 the Asante had conquered the
Fante states which previously had limited their access to Ghana's
coastline. The British, who had negotiated several trading agree-
ments with the Fante people, immediately felt their interests
threatened by this expansion of Asante power. The British sent
several negotiating teams, like the one mentioned above led by
Bowdich, to try to secure a continuation of their commercial activities as well as some measure of political power on Ghana's
coastline.

One particularly unwise British official by the name of Sir
Charles MacCarthy was dissatisfied with the terms of their agree-
ments with the Asante, and used the pretext of the arrest and subsequent execution of a British sergeant to declare war on the
Asante. In the process MacCarthy had attempted to create ferment
in the Asante empire by supporting dissident groupings.

In their first major clash the Asante army annihilated Mac-
Carthy and his British contingent in 1824. At that time the
Asante army numbered 80,000 with about 40,000 having the use
of muskets and blunderbusses. The British quickly learned the
lesson of their defeat by the Asante and replaced MacCarthy with
the more conciliatory George Maclean, who increased British
influence in Ghana by maintaining good relations with the Asante
and concentrated British activities in those areas not under
Asante control. Through Maclean's skilful diplomacy the British
were able to edge out other European traders from Ghana, and in
doing so to help to suppress the slave trade, which had been
banned by a British Act of Parliament in 1807, and to set about
pursuing Britain's more modern colonial objectives – namely, the

5 Nkrumah, *Autobiography*, p. 164.

Nkrumah with Fidel Castro: discussing a document on the non-aligned movement.

Nkrumah: laying the foundation stone at the Gold Coast State House.

Nkrumah with Sekon Toure when the latter visited Ghana.

Nkrumah, the 'Father of the Nation'.

Premier Nkrumah seen addressing thousands of people who attended a 'durbar' in his honour at Yendi.

Nkrumah at the 1961 Republic Day celebrations.

Nkrumah, accompanied by some other Ghanaian Ministers during his state tour to Nigeria.

Nkrumah's wife — Fathia — with their children.

Nkrumah talking intensely with John Tettegah, the trades union leader.

Nkrumah with the late Soviet premier, Nikita Kruschev.

Nkrumah with the late Egyptian leader, Gamel A. Nasser.

Talking to the masses, with Pan African colleague Sekon Toure.

dominance of the commodity trade.

The growth of this influence resulted in the signing of a Bond in 1844 between Ghana's coastal peoples and the British. In essence the Bond laid down the limits of British jurisdiction in Ghana, but with Maclean's death in Ghana in 1847, his British successors increasingly ignored the terms of the 1844 Bond. As Nkrumah pointed out in his 1953 *Motion of Destiny* speech:

> From the humble beginnings of trade and friendship
> [effected by the Bond of 1844], Britain assumed political
> control of this country. As my friend George Padmore puts it
> – 'when the Gold Coast Africans demand self-government
> today they are in consequence merely asserting their birth-
> right which they never really surrendered to the British, who,
> disregarding their treaty obligations of 1844, gradually
> usurped full sovereignty over the country'.[6]

The creeping expansion of British power following the signing of the 1844 Bond and British efforts to raise taxes to cover their commercial costs inevitably led to further clashes with the Asante. The refusal by the British to hand back two fugitives to the Asantehene provided the pretext for the reopening of hostilities between the Asante and the British in 1862. Again the Asante inflicted a series of defeats on the British troops, eventually forcing their ignominious withdrawal. The fiasco of the British defeat almost led to British withdrawal from Ghana. But after much internal debate the British colonial authorities decided to set up 'protectorates' in 1866 ostensibly to protect the coastal peoples from the Asante, although in reality they existed to shore up Britain's position in Ghana.

Far from being seen as protecting anybody from anybody else the growing British influence sparked off a series of protest movements headed by the Fante and Krobo people. The object of these movements was to secure independence from the British and Asante domination. As Nkrumah wrote in 1953:

> The Fante Confederation – the earliest manifestation of
> Gold Coast Nationalism – occurred in 1868 when the Fante
> chiefs attempted to form the Fante Confederation in order to

6 Ibid., p. 164.

defend themselves against the Asante and the incipient encroachments of the British merchants. It was also a union of the coastal states for mutual economic and social development. This was declared a dangerous conspiracy with the consequent arrest of its leaders.

The life-span of the Fante Confederation, which was really a nationalist movement for all the coastal peoples, was all too brief – lasting from 1868 to 1873, when it dissolved under British pressure. It was nevertheless, as Nkrumah pointed out, a movement which stood for the attainment of self-government and 'for the achievement of the social progress of our subjects and people, of education and industrial pursuits'. It was the first movement Ghana had seen where its traditional rulers had joined together with the educated elite to fight for independence in common cause. Many Ghanaians saw it as laying the foundations for the late Aborigines Rights Protection Society and ultimately the United Gold Coast Convention of which Nkrumah became Secretary-General on his return from Britain in 1948.

The British seized the opportunity of the collapse of the Fante Confederation and the withdrawal of the Dutch to entrench themselves further in Ghana. In 1874 the British decisively defeated the now tottering Asante empire, which was already wrecked by internal dissension. Despite their victory, the British authorities were not keen to annex Asante territory because of what they saw as the limited economic returns on such a venture. And at first, having noted the internal problems among the Asante peoples, the British reasoned that there was no need to annex their territory in an operation that would be costly in terms of men and material resources. But at the same time the British could not ignore the wider implications of the Europeans' scramble for Africa, which had far more to do with the rival claims of Europeans within their own continent than any particularly well-thought-out strategy towards Africa.

In reality, the Berlin Conference achieved practically nothing. It was merely one step in a process that was already well under way and the recognition that Europe's colonial policy would continue to be dictated by its increasing mercantile interest. The ego boost that colonialism gave to the Europeans' national pride would continue to be of secondary importance to the main policy-makers, at least!

So the Berlin Conference neither started nor even really managed to regulate the partition of Africa, because in each area of Africa the colonialists had adopted differing strategies according to the balance of European forces in evidence and the balances of African forces which they confronted.

Fortunately, the Ghanaians had consistently managed to confront the European traders and then the British colonialists with organised societies and militia, which had prevented wholesale invasion of their territories. The British attitude to the Asante was a case in point: for almost twenty years after their victory against the Asante, the British government refused pressures from its officials to annex the Asante territory both out of respect for the Asante people and in view of the burden of the cost that it would entail. But in 1895, with a change of personnel at the Colonial Office in London, the policy changed and a British column marched on Kumasi, sacked the town and sent the best of the royal treasures to London. They demanded a £175,000 indemnity from the Asante-hene, King Prempeh I, who was unable to pay and was shipped off to Sierra Leone. Having captured Kumasi, the British were able to take over Ghana's northern states with relative ease.

Chapter 3

Young Nkrumah Goes Abroad

> The only certain facts about my birth appear to be that I was born in the village of Nkroful in Nzima around midday on a Saturday in mid-September.[1]

According to his mother, Nyaniba, Kwame Nkrumah was born in 1912, although the Roman Catholic priest who baptised him puts the date at 1909. In any event, this future leader of Ghana was born at a turning point in his country's history. Little more than ten years before Nkrumah's birth the British had defeated the Asante and sent their leader, the Asantehene, into exile. Ghana was now a fully fledged British colony and was accordingly renamed the Gold Coast.

The more thoughtful British colonisers would have been able to realise that this colonisation process was to be a hollow victory for them. For even as colonialism was being established, the seeds for its destruction were being sown by movements like the Fante Confederation of 1871 and the Aborigines Rights Protection Society established in 1897. At the same time the young nationalist movement was publishing a range of newspapers – the *Gold Coast News*, the *Gold Coast Times*, the *Gold Coast People*, and, most significantly, the *Gold Coast Independent* – which were at first restricted to promoting the cause of nationalism among Ghana's growing professional class.

Moreover, just as significantly for Nkrumah, on the international level the rapid growth in educational opportunities and improve-

1 Nkrumah, *Autobiography*, p. 1.

ment in communications in the nineteenth century had laid the groundwork for the development of an effective Pan-African movement. Afro-American writers and activists like Booker T. Washington and William DuBois had led the fight against racism in the USA. They had been fortified by the belief that the way forward for all black people was to unite under the banner of Pan-Africanism – whether their struggle was in Africa, Europe or America. At the first Pan-African Conference held in London in 1900, the word 'Pan-African' entered the international lexicon of politics – and it is the word that is the key to Nkrumah's political philosophy. Forty-five years after that first Pan-African Conference, Nkrumah was to address that same body also in England, this time in the city of Manchester, saying:

> We believe in the rights of all peoples to govern themselves.
> We affirm the right of all colonial peoples to control their
> destiny. All colonies must be free from foreign imperialist
> control, whether political or economic. The peoples of the
> colonies must have the right to elect their own government, a
> government without restrictions from a foreign power. We
> say to the peoples of the colonies that they must strive for
> these ends by all means at their disposal. The fifth Pan-
> African Congress calls on the workers and farmers of the
> colonies to organise effectively. Colonial workers must be in
> the front lines of the battle against imperialism. The fifth
> Pan-African Congress calls on the intellectuals and profes-
> sional classes to awaken to their responsibilities. The long,
> long night is over. Today there is only one road to effective
> action – the organisation of the masses.[2]

The emergence of Nkrumah as a great Pan-African leader may have seemed unlikely back in his village of Nkroful at the beginning of the twentieth century. The transition from a small boy who early on in his life became obsessed with books and ideas to become a formidably good schoolroom teacher and then on to become the President of his country in no way seemed obvious or inevitable. His upbringing was simple but he was cared for and loved by his family. And importantly for that time, when barely 5 per cent of

2 Nkrumah, *Towards Colonial Freedom*, Appendix p. 44.

27

Ghanaians went to school, Nkrumah's parents, illiterates themselves, were determined to see him get an education.

Nkrumah's father was a goldsmith, rich enough to bring up
several children – with several different wives – but he was not of
the traditional aristocracy. Indeed, because of his simple
upbringing in a traditional African village, Nkrumah can be truly
said to be a leader born of the people. The experiences and aspirations of the poor masses of Africa, as well as the love and affection
they have within them, imprinted themselves on Nkrumah's mind
from the first. It was his upbringing that always brought him down
to earth when the obstacles appeared to be too many and the tide of
the events seemed to have turned against him.

Nkrumah's mother was a trader, adding to the family's income by
selling commodities like rice and sugar. As Nkrumah was her only
child, she took special care of him, taking him round on her trips to
buy goods from the various markets in Ghana and the Ivory Coast.
Nkrumah's mother would frequently take him to Half Assini, a
coastal town some 50 km from Nkroful. Mother and son walked all
the way, which took them six days there and back. Half Assini was
separated from the Ivory Coast, then a French colony, by the Tano
River, but Nkrumah's Nzima people lived on both sides of the
border. So Nyaniba would take Nkrumah across into the Ivory
Coast, but instead of bothering with the border posts they would
just get in a boat and sail around the coast. Nkrumah said it was
experiences like these which showed him the absurdity of the
colonial divisions of Africa, when his own family had been divided
by an arbitrary boundary.

The First World War broke out in Europe in 1914, and it was a
war in which Africa was very much on the side-lines. The Europeans were happy to conscript African soldiers into their respective armies, but they saw no contradiction in the Africans fighting
for European freedom while living under the yoke of European
colonialism. Ghanaians served with distinction in a Gold Coast
regiment in a campaign against German Togoland and the Cam-
eroons and later in German East Africa. After Germany's defeat, its
African colonies were divided up among the Allies in the form of a
mandate granted by the League of Nations. Once again the map of
Africa was being redrawn by people who were totally unconcerned
about the interests and opinions of Africans.

At the time these events hardly touched young Nkrumah, who

was just starting his formal education in a Roman Catholic mission school. Nkrumah soon developed as an all-rounder – a voracious reader and debater, and also a competent athlete – and won the popularity of his peers. At the age of seventeen Nkrumah finished the school curriculum, but the school retained him as a pupil teacher, and from the first he excelled as a teacher – so much so that when the principal of the prestigious Achimota College in Accra, the Reverend A. G. Fraser, visited Nkrumah's school at Half Assini in 1926 and saw this young man teaching pupils who were not much younger than himself, he immediately recommended that Nkrumah should come to Accra to study further at Achimota.

At the time Achimota was one of the few secondary schools in Africa to compare with the best anywhere in Europe or America. It was built on the instructions of the British governor, Sir Gordon Guggisburg, a liberal who believed that the betterment of conditions for Africans was the key to resolving the continuing conflict between coloniser and colonised. The Colonial Office in London had opposed Guggisburg's plans for Achimota, arguing that education for Africans would be disruptive in the colonies – and they were of course correct, for the education of Kwame Nkrumah was to prove very disruptive to colonial rule! What the colonial authorities did not realise was that if they tried to stop it, Africans would find means and access to the education and knowledge they needed to overthrow colonialism come what may.

Nkrumah stayed at Achimota for four years and it was clearly a formative experience in his life. The school had attractive grounds and housing for the students and staff, a museum, a swimming pool, a demonstration farm and a model village. Most of the senior teachers had Oxbridge degrees, and Nkrumah's admission there – by stroke of good fortune – placed him among the most privileged of the African youth of his time.

Coming to Accra to study at Achimota affected Nkrumah on several levels. He had left the quiet rural life at Half Assini for the urban hustle and bustle of Accra, and at first he was remorselessly teased by his peers, born and bred in Accra, for being a country bumpkin. It was here that Nkrumah first saw the deep divisions between Africa's cities and rural areas, and at the same time he gained a clearer idea of the social class divisions in the society. Most of his contemporaries at Achimota had come from the same humble circumstances as Nkrumah.

One of the men who helped Nkrumah make sense of the changing face of Ghana and Africa was the vice-principal at Achimota, Dr Kwegyr Aggrey, under whom Nkrumah took a course in African studies. Aggrey had a profound influence on Nkrumah, who describes the man in his autobiography:

> To me Aggrey seemed the most remarkable man I had ever met and I had the deepest affection for him. He possessed intense vitality and enthusiasm and a most infectious laugh that seemed to bubble up from his heart, and he was a great orator. It was through him that my nationalism was first aroused. He was extremely proud of his color, but he was opposed to racial segregation of any kind.[3]

From Nkrumah's descriptions of Aggrey, he indeed seemed to be a remarkable man – a knowledgeable and generous teacher who was neither pompous nor patronising towards his pupils. Nkrumah relates the last time he saw Aggrey:

> He was brimming over with life and excited about his leave which he was spending in England and America. He stayed and joked with us for a time and then just as he was about to leave, his mood became serious as he said 'Brothers pray for me. So far I have been able to make you hungry but I have not been able to satisfy your hunger. Pray for me that when I come back I may be able to satisfy your hunger.'[4]

The tragedy was that Aggrey never did come back. After visiting friends in England he travelled on to New York where he fell seriously ill and died. Deeply upset by the loss of a man who was a dear friend and mentor, Nkrumah vowed to uphold the spirit of Aggrey – both by forcefully arguing for the man's principles and by resolving to further his education to enable him to put those principles into action. Aggrey might best be remembered for his straightforward statement of principle: 'Only the best is good enough for Africa' – a powerful statement of conviction that today's leaders would do well to remember.

3 Nkrumah, *Autobiography*, p. 12.
4 Ibid., p. 12.

Aggrey's spirit was also remembered by the activities of the Aggrey Students' Society, the debating society which was formed at Achimota in his honour. And it was at this debating society that Nkrumah established his skills of argument that were able to make him the formidable political leader he became. Nkrumah was never to be a truly great orator – he didn't have the voice or carriage for it – but he had the highly developed skills of political persuasion that made him compelling to listen to. He would delight in taking an unpopular view in the debating society and marshal his arguments accordingly.

In 1930 he graduated from Achimota and was immediately confronted with the necessity of earning a living. Typically, Nkrumah had argued with the local Roman Catholic Bishop at Elimina, although this did not stop him being employed as a primary school teacher at the local Roman Catholic junior school. In this, his first formal teaching appointment, he was a popular and effective teacher and, again typically, apart from his teaching duties, he still found time to found the Teachers Association, a trade-union organisation aimed at bettering the working conditions of Ghana's teachers.

Within a year he was promoted to head teacher at the Roman Catholic junior school at Axim, and in his spare time he studied for the entrance examinations for London University. Although he was unsuccessful here, he was still determined to travel out of Ghana for his further education and a university education in America became his goal. In the meantime he went to teach at a Roman Catholic seminary at Amissano near Elmina, which at the time was a new institution and the first time the Roman Catholic Church had established such a place in the country to train its own clergy. Nkrumah said he was somewhat bemused by his appointment to the job; he thought it might be the Church's way of attracting a straying sheep back to the fold. In one respect the Church authorities were right, for during his time at the seminary, Nkrumah had to obey the rules of the institution and said that he regained some of the religious fervour of his earlier years to the extent that he seriously considered joining the priesthood himself.

Nkrumah's attraction to the contemplative and spiritual aspects of religion, combined with his zeal for social reform, made it particularly difficult to describe his world view. He once described himself as a 'non-denominational Christian and a Marxian Socialist' – a combination that might worry both the communists and the Christians, but interestingly, it is a combination that one hears much of in the Third World, particularly among the radical priests in Latin America who have little difficulty in joining the claims of Christianity and socialism together in the fight for liberation.

However, while he was at the seminary, Nkrumah's nationalism was kept alive by writers and activists such as the Nigerian Nnamdi Azikiwe, who championed the cause of African nationalism in a newspaper called the *African Morning Post*. Azikiwe, himself a graduate from an American university, was an inspiration to the other nationalists. Together with the Sierra Leonean nationalist, Wallace Johnson, he campaigned against colonialism and ridiculed European rule in Africa. Azikiwe constantly faced the wrath of the colonial authorities for his writings and agitation. Both Johnson and Azikiwe were prosecuted for sedition after the publication of an article entitled 'Has the African a God?', which appeared in the *African Morning Post* in 1936:

> Personally I believe the European has a God in whom he believes and whom he is representing in his churches all over Africa. He believes in the god whose name is spelt deceit. He believes in the god whose law is 'Ye strong, you Europeans, you must civilise the barbarous Africans with machine guns. Ye Christian Europeans, you must 'christian-ise' the pagan Africans with bombs, poison gases, etc.[5]

While Azikiwe was prosecuted for sedition as a result of the above, Nkrumah noted at the same time that the sentiments were the 'first warning puff of smoke that a fire had been lit, a fire that would prove impossible to extinguish'.[6]

The United States

Nkrumah's voyage to the United States started with a trip to Nigeria. Not having a scholarship to the American university of his

5 Ibid., p. 19.
6 Ibid., p. 21.

choice, he had to raise the money through independent means. That meant saving from his meagre salary as a teacher and relying, like most Africans, on the friendship and generosity of his family. Accordingly, the first length of his voyage to America was a stowaway trip to Lagos, where he went to see a wealthy uncle who helped him with the funding for his main voyage to Britain and the United States.

Once on the main voyage from Takoradi to Liverpool, Nkrumah describes in his autobiography how he suddenly felt alone sitting on his bunk 'close to tears' as he realised he was leaving his beloved Africa for the first time. But he mentions that a few kind words from his friend Azikiwe helped to spur him on. 'Goodbye. Remember to trust in God and yourself,' was the message Azikiwe had sent Nkrumah in a farewell telegram.

Nkrumah arrived in England as Europe was gearing itself up for its second major war this century, as the German fascists were planning to move across Central Europe and strike at the Soviet Union, and the Italian fascists under 'Il Duce' Benito Mussolini had already started their colonial adventures. 'Mussolini invades Ethiopia!', read the headlines, but Nkrumah was shocked to find that the apparently impassive British appeared to be totally unconcerned by this turn of events. It seemed they had neither the time nor the interest in the victims of colonialism and fascism.

Having got his American visa at the US Embassy in London – in those days there was no American diplomatic representation in the Gold Coast – Nkrumah boarded a Cunard White Star liner to New York. Ghana's future leader arrived in the United States in inauspicious circumstances: he had virtually exhausted his funds during the passage, did not even have a definite place at a university, and was two months late for the start of term. Before leaving Ghana, he had written to the Dean of Lincoln University in Pennsylvania, who could not help but admire Nkrumah's determination. Nkrumah's application to Lincoln University, dated 1 March 1935, quoted Tennyson's 'In Memoriam':

> So many worlds,
> So much to do,
> So little done,
> Such things to be.[7]

7 A. B. Assensoh, *Kwame Nkrumah: Six Years in Exile.*

On meeting him the Dean duly admitted the young Ghanaian on condition that he excelled in the forthcoming freshman (first year) examinations. Nkrumah did do well and duly received a scholarship. But the money problems remained, and for almost his entire academic career in America, Nkrumah was compelled to pay for his studies and other expenses by working part-time. At the time scholarship students at Lincoln were allowed to supplement their payments from the university by working either in the dining hall, or as assistants in the library. Nkrumah jumped at the chance to work in the library, and for some time earned his money in this way, as well as 'ghosting' academic papers for some of the less able but wealthier students. But in the long university holidays there were no such provisions made for students and Nkrumah had to venture out into the wide and sometimes unfriendly world of an America hit by the Great Depression. The jobs varied; sometimes he had to carry animal offal around for delivery to a soap factory, sometimes he worked as a waiter on board ships. Just like his upbringing among the people of Nkroful, Nkrumah's working experience in the United States helped to keep him in touch with the daily struggles of the people – whether they happened to be in the supposedly sophisticated Western societies of the United States and Britain or in colonial Africa. In 1939 he graduated as a bachelor of arts with his major in economics and sociology.

On page 29 of Lincoln University's *Yearbook*, a brief biography of Nkrumah appears underneath two rather boyish-looking photographs of him – in one of which he is wearing a bowler hat. Part of the biography reads:

> Africa's Nwia Kofi (Nkrumah was known in his student days as Francis Nwia-Kofi Nkrumah) conditioned all his intellectual endeavours through his zeal for knowledge. As a freshman he quite easily and interestingly adjusted himself to Lincoln and the new environment, and graduated to a fine and polished gentleman intent on the economic resurrection of his beloved native land.[8]

In the same year a verse about him appeared in the class yearbook:

> Africa is the beloved of Nkrumah's dreams:
> Philosopher, thinker with forceful schemes

8 *Lincoln University Yearbook*, p. 29.

In aesthetics, politics he's in the field,
Nkrumah 'très intéressant' radiates appeal.[9]

No sooner had he gained his degree than Nkrumah enrolled for a master's in theology at Lincoln University, where he could support himself through teaching work. He also gained admission to the University of Pennsylvania for a master's course in education and philosophy. Other students and lecturers remarked on Nkrumah's facility for pursuing two or more degree courses at the same time. But, according to records of the time, few saw Nkrumah as a potential political leader. If they saw him as a leader at all, it seems they thought him more likely to become a religious leader. Dr Paul Kuehner, Registrar of Lincoln University, described Nkrumah as:

> a good student with limitations in ability at points in higher college work. Loved controversy. Quiet. Usually withheld his opinions except in debate (on the team). An eager questioner in class. Critical of any criticism of Great Britain, especially by a non-subject. Held strong views. (His concept of primitive man for example).[10]

Another lecturer at Lincoln, Dr Miller, wrote of Nkrumah at the time:

> Courteous, somewhat aloof. Very religious; led prayer services and tended other facets conscientiously. Good student. Over-dogmatic on certain points of social anthropology. Was Dr Johnson's 'ace boy' in History and Philosophy. (Deeply) embittered by some indeterminate cause late in his seminary year.[11]

After Lincoln Nkrumah would have preferred to read journalism at New York's Columbia University, for this was an era when journalism was seen as a vital means of galvanising through the nationalist press the struggle against colonialism.
At the same time Nkrumah was broadening his reading further, avidly going through the classic works of Kant, Descartes, Schopenhauer, Nietzsche and Freud. In line with the political

9 R. McKowan, *Nkrumah*, New York, Doubleday, 1973, p. 28.
10 Ibid.
11 Ibid.

preferences of the American universities, Nkrumah's reading list still showed a heavy bias towards the idealist philosophers and the relatively new social science of psychoanalysis. There does not seem to be much evidence that Nkrumah was yet reading the works of the radical materialist philosophers like Marx, Plekhanov or Lenin. Instead of the socialist writers, Nkrumah was more interested at this time in the various African and black nationalist writers led by DuBois and Marcus Garvey. Finding himself in sympathy with nationalist aims – out of philosophical conviction and having had the bitter experiences of British and American racism – Nkrumah was drawn to this circle. In particular he was a fervent advocate of Garvey's Pan-Africanism; living in the United States of America had only deepened his desire to work for a United States of Africa. Nkrumah taught black history at the University of Philadelphia, which to his disappointment had to focus on the black community in America, rather than tracing that community back to Africa. So, in order to supplement this curriculum Nkrumah set up an African Studies section, organising an African students' association as a place for meeting and debate. This signalled Nkrumah's entry into politics in America: the association published a journal called the *African Interpreter*, which attempted, according to Nkrumah, to 'revive a spirit of nationalism'.[12] The *African Interpreter* did more than revive a spirit of nationalism. It also managed to incense some of America's more conservative academics. Its inaugural message to its readership struck an immediate blow for Pan-Africanism:

> Fellow Africans – Greetings:
> The future of our country, like the future of most countries throughout the world, lies at stake today. Only action will remove the threat to oppressor and oppressed alike. The cause of Africans everywhere is one with the cause of all peoples of African descent throughout the world. . . Unity, Freedom, Independence, Democracy – these should be our watchwords, our ideals, and not the barbaric totalitarianism of the fascists or the perverted colonial democracy of the imperialists.[13]

12 Nkrumah, *Autobiography*, p. 36.
13 Nkrumah, *Towards Colonial Freedom*.

Introducing himself and his colleagues, Nkrumah refers to the authors of the *African Interpreter* as the 'merchants of light'. But although Lincoln University Theological Seminary's Dean Johnson admired Nkrumah very much, seeing him as 'a deeply religious student', he was shocked by a report in the *African Interpreter* that Nkrumah and some student members of the African Association had visited the grave of Dr Kwegyr Aggrey of Achimota College and, instead of praying to God for the repose of Aggrey's soul, Nkrumah poured a libation, calling on the gods of Africa to assist Aggrey. Johnson dashed off a letter of criticism to Nkrumah, who replied in characteristic style:

> The burden of my life is to live in such a way that I may become a living symbol of all that is best both in Christianity and in the laws, customs and beliefs of my people. I am a Christian and will remain so, but never a blind Christian.[14]

This episode marks the beginning of Nkrumah's progressive disenchantment with the American authorities, who had begun to realise that they were not merely dealing with a polite and studious African who had come to America to study and better himself, but that this man held strong opinions and was not afraid to air them and argue with them all. At the same time Nkrumah was increasingly seeing the appalling conditions that the American poor, particularly the blacks, lived in amidst the material splendour of the middle and upper classes, members of which he had met in the country's academic institutions. A local Presbyterian church commissioned him to carry out a survey of the living conditions of the local black population. Nkrumah was appalled by what he saw and heard, about the poverty and discrimination that was the daily lot of so many of America's black population. Accordingly, he expanded his reading to include some of the Marxist classics, although, according to the Trinidadian writer C. L. R. James, Nkrumah did not show that these works had given him a clear guide to action. Rather, Nkrumah seems to have learned two more fundamental lessons from his struggle in America: hard work and organisation are required to get anywhere in life.

14 Ibid.

Nkrumah was invited with growing frequency to speak at public meetings in the United States, mostly about Africa: the rights and wrongs of colonialism, the ancient African kingdoms and the essential unity of black Americans and Africans. These lectures often challenged the conventional views of European anthropologists about Africa. As a result of these public engagements, Nkrumah's stature in America grew and he met many prominent black activists – like C. L. R. James, who helped Nkrumah on the next stage of his career by writing a letter to the Trinidadian radical George Padmore, who was at the time living in London.

London

C. L. R. James's contact with Padmore had set in train a series of letters between Nkrumah and Padmore about the anti-colonial movement and wider issues of how to bring about socialism in Africa. So it was natural for Padmore to receive Nkrumah on his arrival in London from America. Padmore met Nkrumah at London's Victoria Station, and to his delight took him straight to the headquarters of the West African Students' Union, which was organised to help African students abroad. Nkrumah had come to London both to study and to join the burgeoning anti-colonial movement. It was a momentous time. The Second World War had just ended, and a spirit of radicalism had swept Britain during the privations of wartime which had resulted in the election of a Labour government which had clearly expressed itself sympathetic to the ambitions of the colonial peoples.

There was, too, the growing power of the anti-colonial movement led by Gandhi and Nehru. It was the experience of living and working in these times that helped Nkrumah to see the importance of unity among all the peoples of the colonies, regardless of their race.

Academically Nkrumah wanted to read for his philosophy doctorate at the London School of Economics, under the eminent professor Sir Alfred Ayer, and then to enrol at the Inns of Court to study law. He started off both these academic projects, but was brought into the thick of the preparations for the fifth Pan-

Africanist Congress to be held in Manchester the October after his arrival. Nkrumah worked ceaselessly with the more experienced Padmore in writing letters to African organisations in Africa and the Caribbean, urging them to send delegations and contributions to the Congress.

Indeed, the fifth Pan-Africanist Congress turned out to be a watershed in the history of the movement: the key activists attended. Besides Nkrumah, there was Jomo Kenyatta; the South African novelist, Peter Abrahams; the poet from Togo, Raphael Armatta; and Sierra Leone trade unionist and journalist, Wallace Johnson. The Congress explicitly condemned colonialism as a systematic exploitation of the economic resources of the domi- nated countries and was also explicit in its demands for 'one man, one vote', which was a shocking idea for the old-style colonial administrations.

After the Congress, fired by the enthusiasm of the delegates, Nkrumah published his first collection of essays, *Towards Colonial Freedom*, with titles like 'Colonialism and Imperialism', 'Colonial Economics', 'Apology for Apologetics' and 'Colonial Policies: Theory and Practice'. The essays contain a theoretical analysis of the situation in the colonies and are strong on slogans, rather than giving the clear programme of action to be taken against colonial- ism that the title of the volume would suggest:

> The national liberation movement in the African colonies
> has arisen because of the continuous economic and political
> exploitation by foreign oppressors. The aim of the move-
> ment is to win freedom and independence. This can only be
> achieved by the political education and organisation of the
> colonial masses. Hence workers and professional classes
> alike must unite on a common front to further the economic
> progress and indigenous enterprise of the people which is at
> present being stifled.[15]

At the same time Nkrumah was trying to formulate a more specific political programme for a thoroughgoing anti-colonial movement in Ghana in particular, and for the African continent as a whole. To

15 Ibid.

this end, he started a small political sect called 'The Circle', which aimed to work as the 'revolutionary vanguard of the struggle for West African Freedom and Independence'. The Circle was essentially a clandestine movement whose members correctly believed that they would be persecuted on their return to their home countries.

While Nkrumah's theoretical perspectives and organisational skills were developing, there were clear limits to what he could achieve in practice so far away from home. As he knew he had to return to Ghana to become part of the growing anti-colonial movement there, it was no surprise that he decided to take up an offer made to him by an old friend, Ako Adjei.

Chapter 4

A Nation in Wait for a Tribune

In the history of a nation there comes a time when the people become aware of the necessity for far-reaching change. It was precisely at such a moment, on 19 December 1947, that Kwame Nkrumah landed in Takoradi. The Ghana which Nkrumah had left in the thirties was not the Ghana to which he returned. The people were tired of colonial rule. Throughout the land an atmosphere of excitement, anticipating freedom, was evident. Ghana was ready to fight.

The new climate of resistance was shaped by the experience of the previous decade. During the Second World War, life in colonial Ghana was disrupted, never to return to the era of relative stability. The Western Allies themselves raised the banner of freedom in an attempt to win the support of the colonial people for their war effort. Expectations of freedom in exchange for sacrifices in war were high. Thousands of Ghanaian soldiers had fought abroad. The experience was crucial in opening their eyes to the ways of the world. Mixing with other Africans and with Asians, they could see that throughout the Third World there was a common yearning for freedom. Many had come into direct contact with activists of the Indian liberation struggle. When the ex-servicemen returned to Ghana they were no longer content to go back to their old way of life. Radicalised by their experience, the ex-soldiers went around telling others what they had seen.

If the ex-soldiers were discontented, so were the people they had left behind. During the war, people suffered major economic hardship. There were severe shortages of foodstuffs. The difficulties of finding food were compounded by the high prices charged for the

41

basics of life. There were many merchants who were happy to manipulate the market and make large profits by raising the prices of much-needed goods. Dissatisfaction was widespread. During the war thousands of Ghanaians left the villages for the towns. As people from one region mixed with those of another, news travelled quickly. Through the markets, rumours and information spread from one corner of the country to another. The markets became a hive of information and political discussion. Ghana did not need politicians to tell people what they wanted. A widespread yearning for a better life is clearly expressed in a petition addressed to the Governor of the Gold Coast Ex-Servicemen's Union on 28 February 1948. The petition made the following points:[1]

1 Failure on the part of the government to implement promises made to ex-servicemen when they were in the army.

2 Insufficiency of disablement pension rates having regard to the increased cost of living.

3 Grants to men too old to enter the government service and to men anxious to start business on their own account had not been made, as was done in the United Kingdom.

4 Provisions should be made exempting all ex-servicemen from payment of state levies for a period of five years.

5 Army training in vocational work was not treated as adequate for civilian or government employment of the same kind upon demobilisation.

6 That when servicemen were demobilised and entered government service, full credit was not given by the establishment for the period of service in the army.

7 Africanisation of the Royal West African Frontier Force was not being effectively maintained, and more African officers were to be granted commissions in the army and non-commissioned officers were to be encouraged to the King's commission.

More widely, workers, peasants and intellectuals agitated for lower prices, better education and for freedom from colonial domination. This was the Ghana that greeted Nkrumah on his return.

1 Nkrumah, *Autobiography.*

Emergence of the People's Tribune

It was the main nationalist organisation, the United Gold Coast Convention, that invited Kwame Nkrumah to return to Ghana. Founded in 1946, the UGCC was led by Dr Danquah, Nkrumah's future bitter political enemy. The UGCC was officially launched in 1947. Its main demand was that of 'self-government for the peoples of the Gold Coast at the earliest opportunity'. The UGCC was a nationalist movement, but it was a movement led by lawyers and businessmen who were out of touch with the feelings of the people. The UGCC lacked organisation and an inclination to mobilise the masses. It was a nationalist movement without mass support. Aware of their political isolation, the leaders of the UGCC looked for someone to organise and popularise the Convention. This was why the UGCC turned to Nkrumah and appointed him as its national organiser.

Nkrumah spent the first fortnight back in Ghana finding out the mood of the country and working out plans for the future. Once he became aware of the widespread popular desire for change he moved swiftly. He set up an office in Saltpond and began to work out the organisational proposals necessary for building an effective mass movement. On 20 January 1948 he called a meeting of the Working Committee of the Convention and laid before it a programme of action. The importance of this programme for the future of Ghana cannot be overestimated. For the first time a clear plan directed towards the objective of national independence was put before the people.

Nkrumah's programme of January 1948 consisted of three phases. For the first period, Nkrumah argued for a vigorous policy of organisation and mobilisation. The UGCC would seek to co-ordinate and win affiliation from all existing political, social, educational, farmers' and women's organisations. It would go out and set up branches of the UGCC in every town and village of the country. A thorough programme of political education would be initiated to consolidate all party branches and to prepare the country for self-government. This process of mass organisation and mobilisation would be followed by the second period, which would 'be marked by constant demonstrations throughout the country to test our organisational strength, making use of political crises'. These demonstrations would be a prelude to the third period, which, according to Nkrumah, would consist of:

(a) The convening of a Constitutional Assembly of the Gold Coast people to draw up the Constitution of Self-Government or National Independence.

(b) Organised demonstration, boycott and strike – our only weapons to support our pressure for self-government.[2]

It is a testimony to Nkrumah's vision that the objectives of this three-stage programme were realised in less than two and a half years. Back in January 1958 there were few political leaders who believed that the objective of national independence would be realised so swiftly. No sooner did the UGCC accept the programme of action than Nkrumah set out to implement it. Throughout the next half year Nkrumah travelled up and down the country setting up new branches of the party and preaching the message of freedom. Nkrumah did something that no national leader had attempted hitherto. He went to the villages, talked to ordinary people and gave the masses confidence in their ability to take control over their lives. Nkrumah later recalled this period as one which:

> called for much intensive travelling. . . . Things might have been a bit better if I had a more reliable car, but the ancient model that was supplied to me rarely finished a journey. It usually meant that I had to leave it with the driver while I continued my trek on foot. Sometimes if a 'mammy' lorry happened to be travelling past I managed to get a lift, but I was not always lucky in this respect. Most of the time I managed to arrange things so that I spent the night in one of the villages, but on several occasions, when I had got stuck too far out in the bush by nightfall, I was obliged to sleep on the roadside.[3]

Travelling like this may have had its discomforts, but it provided an important education for Nkrumah. Through direct contact with the villages, the young nationalist leader learned much about what

2 Ibid., p. 61.
3 Nkrumah, *Towards Colonial Freedom*, p. xiv.

people were thinking, what concerned them, and what were their dreams and hopes. The positive response to Nkrumah's speeches indicated that there was, at least in embryo, an army ready to fight. And Nkrumah through his travels learned what the people wanted and how far they were prepared to go. Most important of all, Nkrumah could now claim to speak not for himself but for a whole people. He was becoming the People's Tribune – a leader well able to articulate clearly what until then had remained the subject of incoherent conversation in the towns and villages. It was for this reason that people attending Nkrumah's rallies so readily recognised themselves as at one with the speaker.

Nkrumah's travels also had immediate practical consequences. Until he embarked on his journey, the UGCC had organised only two active branches. Within six months of Nkrumah's setting out on his travels, the UGCC could boast of more than five hundred branches. Nkrumah organised hundreds of meetings. The tens of thousands who attended went away convinced that they had a responsibility to fight for their nation. It was this conviction that they had something to fight for that motivated thousands to join and become involved. In six months a mass nationalist movement had been created.

The people knew what they wanted, but through Nkrumah they acquired the confidence and the direction for victory. This was a time of tremendous receptivity to effective leadership. The fluidity of the situation can be seen in the mass boycotts of European imported goods which coincided with Nkrumah's organisational drive. On 11 January 1948 a boycott of European imported goods was launched in Accra. Organised by a sub-chief, Nii Kwabena Bonne, in the name of the Anti-Inflation Committee, the boycott represented a protest against high prices. The colonial administration was taken aback by the success of the boycott. It spread throughout the country and enjoyed mass support. In the end it was called off on 28 February, when government officials promised that prices would be reduced.

On the day that the boycott was called off, there occurred an event which was to initiate a new chapter in the history of the anti-colonial resistance in Ghana. The Ex-Servicemen's Union had organised a demonstration to present a petition to the Governor. As the march set off there was little indication of any trouble. But when the march changed the prescribed route so that the ex-servicemen could go directly to Christiansborg Castle, the residence of the Governor, a detachment of police stood in its way. The police commanded the ex-servicemen to halt. The demonstrators protested and insisted on their right to continue their peaceful march. In the heat of the moment, a European police officer fired at the head of the demonstration. Two Africans were killed at once and five others were seriously wounded. But bullets cannot kill a dream. News of the shootings spread throughout Accra, provoking anger and indignation. During the next two days the police lost control as the rioting spread from Accra to all the major towns. In Accra itself, fifteen were killed and 155 were wounded and injured.

The outbreak of mass disturbances furnished clear proof of the anger and determination of the people. Taken aback by the strength of feeling of its subjects, the colonial administration moved into action to contain the unrest. Although the disturbances were unorganised and spontaneous, the colonialists had to find scapegoats. Within two weeks Nkrumah and five other leaders of the UGCC were arrested and imprisoned. They were held for eight weeks, during which time the colonial government attempted to fabricate a case against them. In the end, Nkrumah and the others were let out to minimise the risk of further unrest. The disturbances forced the British to move carefully. A Commission of Inquiry into the disturbances concluded by recommending the enactment of a more democratic constitution for the country. However, Nkrumah had little faith in such commissions. Upon his release, he set out to continue his organisational drive on behalf of the UGCC.

Parting of the Ways

Under Nkrumah's direction the UGCC had become a mass organisation. But this was not to the liking of all the UGCC's leaders. Nkrumah's success was based on his ability to bring workers and peasants into active political life. He gave shape to the grassroots pressure for change and transformed it into a formidable political force. However, the old leadership of the UGCC felt ill at ease with mass politics. As successful lawyers and businessmen, they had acquired the habits and tastes of their colonial masters and looked upon the ordinary people with a degree of contempt. They instinctively recognised that mass mobilisation could also threaten their own privileges and doom them to irrelevance.

Tension between Nkrumah and the rest of the UGCC leadership surfaced in the aftermath of the Christiansborg disturbances. While under arrest, leading UGCC politicians like Danquah, Ofori Atta, Akuffo Addo, Ako Adjei and Obetsebi Lamptey began to blame Nkrumah for their imprisonment and they longed for the cosy atmosphere of the elite committee room where they could scheme and wheel and deal. They looked upon the masses as a dangerous force that could undermine their ability to negotiate with the colonial government. In contrast, Nkrumah understood that the British would not yield to reasoning and cosy chats. He wrote in 1947 in an address to intellectuals:

> Those who formulate the colonial issues in accordance with the false point of view of the colonial powers, who are deluded by the futile promises of 'preparing' colonial peoples for 'self-government', who feel that their imperialist oppressors are 'rational' and 'moral' and will relinquish their 'possessions' if only confronted with the truth of the injustice of colonialism are tragically mistaken.[4]

The elite-orientated nationalist leaders feared the consequences of a mass movement taking to the streets. After their release from prison, the politicians around Danquah began to reassess their position and opted to slow down the pace of events. The lesson drawn by Nkrumah from the events surrounding the disturbances was different: Ghana needed more, not less, organisation and mobilisation.

In the face of a barely concealed hostility of the UGCC executive, Nkrumah set out to consolidate the movement for national independence. One of his first initiatives was to set up the Ghana National College, an educational institution designed to prepare students for the new Ghana. The Ghana National College was not just another college. Many students and teachers had recently been victimised because of their support for what Nkrumah had been doing. The colonial authorities wanted to teach them a lesson they

4 Nkrumah, *Autobiography*, p. 78.

would not forget: they were promptly expelled from their various colleges. It was these refugees from the colonial educational establishments who formed the initial intake of this new college. By its very existence, it became a school of defiance. In his speech which inaugurated the college on 20 July 1948, Nkrumah explained that its main task was to 'liberate the minds of our youth so that they should be ready to tackle the many problems of our time.'[5]

In the meantime the UGCC executive committee, looking for an excuse to cut Nkrumah down to size, attacked him for this initiative. On 3 September, Nkrumah was called before the executive committee and denounced for establishing the Ghana National College without their authority. This was the pretext used to attack Nkrumah for his pursuit of mass politics. Some on the executive proposed his removal while others, fearing the consequences of such blatant victimisation, proposed a compromise. In the end he was demoted to the post of treasurer.

Fortunately for Ghana, Nkrumah did not cave in to the pressure of the UGCC executive. It was realised that there was much more at stake than the bruised egos of a handful of politicians. Instead of giving in, Nkrumah continued to mobilise and to launch his next major initiative, the *Accra Evening News*. Danquah and his colleagues rejected proposals to publish a newspaper, fearing that it would provoke the wrath of the colonial officialdom. Nkrumah nevertheless went ahead. He recalled:

> Personally I failed to see how any liberation movement could
> possibly be without an effective means of broadcasting its
> policy to the rank and file of the people. In the same way as I
> took the initiative over the Ghana College, so I made plans to
> launch a newspaper.[6]

The *Accra Evening News* was an instant success. It was avidly read and discussed on the streets. Groups would gather on street corners and read the contents out to those who were not literate.

However, the most important aspect of Nkrumah's campaign was to organise young people. Nkrumah understood that young people, the most energetic section of the population, had to

5 Ibid., p. 82.
6 Ibid., p. 92.

be won to the cause of the independence movement. He began by establishing the Youth Study Group in Accra and later extended this enterprise by launching the Ghana Youth Association in Sekondi and the Asante Youth Association. Those organisations, directly under Nkrumah's influence, provided him with a power base to deal with the manoeuvres of the UGCC executive. The programme of the Committee on Youth Organisation (CYO) reflected the radical objectives of its founder. It called for 'Self-Government Now', which represented a clear-cut alternative to the UGCC's slogan 'Self-Government within the shortest possible time'.

The working committee of the UGCC rightly saw the well-organised youth movement as a threat to its authority. Danquah and his colleagues decided that the time had come for a split with Nkrumah and his supporters. Throughout the early part of 1949 both sides were busy mobilising their supporters for the coming showdown. At least informally, two political parties were in existence, the working committee of the UGCC and the CYO. But it was not until the CYO held its special conference in Tarkwa in June 1949 that the desire for the establishment of a new radical nationalist party publicly surfaced. On 12 June 1949, after much deliberation, the new party, called the Convention People's Party (CPP), was publicly launched in Accra at a mass rally of sixty thousand.

It is important to understand that the split leading to the emergence of the CPP had nothing to do with personalities. The UGCC and the CPP represented conflicting social forces. The handful of elite politicians who ran the UGCC were not in any hurry. As far as they were concerned, their own privileges came first and an upsurge of mass radicalism represented a potential threat to their position. They looked down with contempt at Nkrumah's youthful supporters and dismissed them as 'verandah boys'. Ordinary working class people, the peasantry and the unemployed did not have the luxury of time. They had no privileges to defend and little to lose. They wanted change and they wanted it in their own lifetime. Regardless of Nkrumah, these powerful pressures for change had enveloped the country. And even if the CPP had not emerged, the UGCC could not have contained the powerful impulse for a new life. The methods and policies of the UGCC were simply not appropriate for the time. What the country needed was a fighting organisation and not an intellectual pressure group.

What the split did was to reveal the narrow, elitist pre-occupations of the UGCC. This became all too clear once the CPP took off and became a dynamic mass force. The very existence of such a force was perceived by Danquah and his friends as a direct threat to their own interests. That is why they spent most of their time attacking the CPP. For in the end the UGCC leaders felt closer to the colonial administration than to the mass movement represented by the CPP.

It is important to realise that the basis for split was not so much differences on political as on organisational questions. There were important political differences, to be sure – particularly in relation to the timing for the achievement of self-government. However, the fundamental issue at stake was organisation. Nkrumah's insistence that 'organisation is everything' represented the death-knell for elite politics. By organising the masses, Nkrumah changed the rules of the game. Politics could no longer be restricted to a handful of lawyers drawing up petitions and arguing about the future behind closed doors. Organisation brought ordinary people into political life and in doing so transformed the very meaning of nationalist politics.

Nkrumah had well understood that it is not individuals who make history. No matter how eloquent and convincing, an individual politician carries little weight with imperialist authorities. It is not individual but mass pressure that yields results. Once organised, a people constitute themselves into a nation – and a nation cannot be fobbed off with vague promises. Without a mass organisation, a nationalist party is like a handful of generals without an army. Nkrumah recognised that without an army the war could not be won. Nkrumah did not only create an army, he also devised a strategy for winning the war. It is the examination of this strategy – that of Positive Action – to which we now turn.

Positive Action

The CPP's slogans of 'freedom' and 'Forward Ever, Backward Never' captured the imagination of the UGCC rank and file and the other politicised sections of Ghanaian society. The six-point programme of the CPP embodied the aspiration for freedom in a straightforward manner. They were as follows:

1 To fight relentlessly by all constitutional means for the achievement of full 'Self-Government NOW' for the chiefs and the people of the Gold Coast.

2 To serve as the vigorous conscious political vanguard for removing all forms of oppression and for the establishment of a democratic government.

3 To serve and maintain the complete unity of the Colony, Asante, Northern Territories and Trans-Volta.

4 To work in the interest of the trade union movement for better conditions of employment.

5 To work for a proper reconstruction of a better Gold Coast in which the people shall have the right to live and to govern themselves as free people.

6 To assist and facilitate in any way possible the realisation of a united and self-governing West Africa.[7]

To implement this programme, Nkrumah argued for positive action: the non-violent mobilisation of the masses against the colonial system. Drawing on the experience of the Indian independence movement, Nkrumah argued that there was little point in playing it by the rules established by the British. All means short of violence were legitimate instruments of positive action – political agitation, strikes, boycotts and non-co-operation. To justify this perspective, Nkrumah recalled that freedom had never been handed to any colonial country on a silver platter; it had been won only after bitter and vigorous struggles. Nkrumah did not advocate action for its own sake. In his speeches during the aftermath of the split, he emphasised that positive action ought to be used when all else had failed. But it was not long before the strategy of Positive Action was put to the test. In October 1949, the Coussey Commission, set up to recommend a more democratic constitution for Ghana, published its report. The report proposed the establishment of municipal councils and increased the number of elected

7 Ibid., p. 93.

Africans on the Executive Council. Although the proposals increased the scope for African representation, it clearly failed to meet the widespread demand for self-government. Everyone in the country watched to see what the reaction of Nkrumah and the CPP would be.

As far as Nkrumah was concerned, the new constitution proposed by the Coussey Commission was a confidence trick, designed to give only the semblance of participation to the African. The CPP moved into action to mobilise public opinion against the new constitution. On 20 November 1949, Nkrumah organised a meeting of over fifty organisations. By involving a cross-section of African opinion, Nkrumah hoped to extend the breadth of opposition to the Coussey Commission. This was achieved; and after debate and discussion the Assembly affirmed that

> The Coussey Report and His Majesty's Government's statement thereon are unacceptable to the country as a whole and that the people of the Gold Coast be granted Dominion Status within the Commonwealth of Nations based on the Statute of Westminster.[8]

Once Nkrumah was convinced that he had the broad consensus of the party behind him he raised the stakes. The executive committee of the CPP authorised Nkrumah to write to the Governor informing him that unless the proposed constitution was modified in line with the resolution of the People's Representative Assembly, the party would embark on a campaign of Positive Action. Moreover, Nkrumah insisted that the campaign of non-co-operation would continue until the British government conceded the right of the people of Ghana to work out their own constitution.

On the same day as the warning was issued, 15 December, the front page of the *Accra Evening News* carried the headline 'The Era of Positive Action Draws Nigh'. 'We were prepared for a showdown', recalled Nkrumah.[9] At a mass rally held at the Accra Arena in the evening, Nkrumah gave the colonial government until 1 January 1950 to respond; after that Positive Action would be declared.

Leading colonial officials realised that their authority was under

8 Ibid., p. 94.
9 Ibid., p. 97.

threat. They combined the tactics of repression and persuasion to contain the challenge posed by Positive Action. The judiciary was mobilised and several CPP newspaper editors were prosecuted. While the court proceedings were going on, leading colonial officials attempted to convince Nkrumah to abandon Positive Action. The Colonial Secretary, R. H. Saloway, met with Nkrumah several times but failed to persuade the nationalist leader to back off from confrontation.

Finally, after it had become crystal clear that the colonial government was not prepared to change its attitude, conflict became inevitable. On 9 January, Nkrumah announced that Positive Action would begin at midnight with a general strike across the nation. The government attempted to confuse matters by making false broadcasts claiming that Positive Action had been called off. A campaign of disinformation was launched to fool people and discourage them from going on strike.

The response of the people to the call for Positive Action was overwhelming. Solidarity was very much in evidence as people stayed at home and brought the country to a standstill. Government offices ceased to function and the shops were empty. In Nkrumah's words, the 'political and the social revolution of Ghana had started'. With the situation threatening to get out of hand it is not surprising that the government reacted fiercely. On 11 January, a state of emergency was declared and a curfew imposed. The repression had now begun in earnest. Newspaper offices were raided and their publications were banned. All political meetings were outlawed. On the streets the colonial police were busy hunting down the activists of the CPP, and the numbers arrested steadily mounted. Special constables, who were expatriates, took the law into their hands, attacking those to whom they took exception.

Despite the government crack-down, the African public continued to resist and fight back. It was not until the arrest of most of the leadership of the CPP on 22 January that the government began to get the situation under control. The next day,Nkrumah himself was arrested, and the first phase of Positive Action came to an end.

The colonial authorities were of the opinion that the detention of Nkrumah and his colleagues would mean the end of the struggle for national independence. Nkrumah's trial was a stage-managed affair, with a predictable outcome. Charged with inciting others to participate in an illegal strike, Nkrumah received two separate sentences of one year each. He also received an extra year for his alleged crime of sedition. The government believed that, with Nkrumah out of circulation, Ghana would return to the stability of the good old days. In this belief they were very much mistaken. Once aroused and mobilised, the people of Ghana had no intention of turning the clock back. During the campaign for Positive Action, the masses acquired a sense of their power. This experience showed that, once organised, the African population had the strength to acquire control over its destiny. Iron bars could not prevent Nkrumah from maintaining his influence on African political opinion. The crowds who congregated outside his prison ensured that Nkrumah would know that he was still very much on their mind. A favourite CPP song to the tune of 'John Brown's Body' made this clear:

> Kwame Nkrumah's body lies a-mouldering in his cell
> But his work goes prospering on.

Triumph in Gaol

Prison can often crush the spirit. Certainly it was that which the prison authorities had in mind for Nkrumah and his fellow CPP leaders. Forced into the degrading conditions that prevailed in the colonial gaols, Nkrumah resolved that though his body was restricted in a cell, his spirit would be free. Nkrumah was sustained in this difficult period by the knowledge that the chain of events which he had helped to set in motion were irresistibly leading towards freedom. From this perspective, imprisonment could be seen as a test, as a period of preparation for the struggles ahead.

Fortunately for Nkrumah, although imprisoned, he was not without contacts on the outside. Before he was locked up he managed to establish an arrangement with his colleague, Komla Gbedemah, whereby important information could be communicated between the two. Nkrumah threw his full authority behind Gbedemah and made him responsible for publishing the *Evening News* and for running the CPP. Through Gbedemah, Nkrumah was able to keep up with new events and even influence the development of the CPP. More importantly, the knowledge that the CPP was making progress throughout Ghana greatly strengthened Nkrumah's resolve to fight. Instead of breaking the man, the colonial authorities helped to create a symbol of resistance. As events were to prove, Nkrumah was no less dangerous in prison than outside.

During the first year of his imprisonment, Nkrumah never stopped thinking about the future of the nationalist movement. His energies were absorbed in the difficult task of influencing the strategy of the CPP. His attention was preoccupied with the general election scheduled for 8 February 1951. Nkrumah understood that this election could become an important trial of strength between the CPP and the colonial government. If the CPP could win substantial popular support at the polls, then it would expose the lack of legitimacy of the existing political order to the whole world. It would vindicate the political prisoners like Nkrumah and indict the colonial government. Accordingly, Nkrumah gave instructions to his trusted colleagues that every effort had to be made to win the coming elections. He insisted that every seat had to be contested so that there could be no doubt about the CPP's claim to being the representative of the nation.

Nkrumah also fought a separate legal battle to put himself forward as a candidate. In offering himself as a candidate, Nkrumah sought to demonstrate that his prison sentence was unjust and that he still enjoyed the support of African opinion. After much legal wrangling, Nkrumah managed to stand as the CPP candidate for Accra Central. As the day approached, everyone knew that this was to be more than just another election. It would give a verdict on whether or not the people of Ghana were ready to continue the strategy of Positive Action. Although cut off from the people, Nkrumah the political prisoner was convinced that the future belonged to his movement. He was not mistaken. Soon after the closing of polls, news arrived that Nkrumah was elected for Accra Central. He received the largest poll recorded in the history of the colony: 22,780 votes out of 23,122. The CPP won 34 out of 38 seats in the Legislative Assembly. In contrast, the UGCC was humiliated with only 3 Assembly seats.

The results of the 1951 general election represented the high point of four years of struggle. It confirmed what everyone already knew. It showed that popular resistance to colonialism was no passing episode. The elections also destroyed the legitimacy of the Coussey Constitution. After all, if the bitter opponents of the constitution received such a widespread popular mandate, then clearly the existing political framework lacked legitimacy. And how could anyone have faith in a judiciary system that had branded as a criminal the most popular leader in the land? The game was up and the colonial authorities knew it. The colonial Governor, Sir Arden-Clarke, summarised the situation in the following terms:

> Nkrumah and his Party had the mass of the people behind them and there was no other party with appreciable public support to which one could turn. Without Nkrumah, the Constitution would be still-born and if nothing came of all the hopes, aspirations, and concrete proposals for a greater measure of self-government, there would no longer be any faith in the good intentions of the British Government and the Gold Coast would be plunged into disorders, violence and bloodshed.[10]

What Arden-Clarke meant in effect was that, without Nkrumah, Ghana could not be governed.

Recognising political realities, the Governor had Nkrumah released from prison the day after the election results were announced. Next day the former convict was sitting across the table from the Governor, discussing the future of Ghana. When he left the meeting he had in his pocket authorisation to form a government. Yesterday's prisoner had become the leading parliamentarian in Ghana.

Nkrumah was not one to let success go to his head. Even in this hour of triumph he understood that the CPP's election victory still fell short of the achievement of self-government. The constitution was far from democratic and the most important decisions were still subject to the veto of the colonial authorities. In his address to the new CPP Assembly, Nkrumah went to great lengths to alert them to the dangers of working under the existing constitution. He stated that going to the Assembly is 'not an end, but a means whereby "self-government now" can be fought for and won, both from within and from without the Assembly'.[11] The risks were high in endowing this

10 Ibid.
11 Ibid., p. 115.

56

institution with legitimacy. On the other hand, if the CPP had boy-cotted it, there was the danger that other African politicians more pliable to colonial pressure would breathe life into the Legislative Assembly. Whether or not Nkrumah and the CPP made the right decision would become clear in the next few years ahead.

Chapter 5

The Painful Transition

By all rights the 1951 general election should have settled matters once and for all. The people had made their position clear: they wanted independence immediately. The British officials in Ghana knew that independence could not be indefinitely postponed. What they wanted was time – time to organise and time to strengthen their hold over Ghana. This was the real meaning of the term 'transfer of power'. Power can never be transferred. It is not divisible; you either wield it or you do not. The aim of 'transferring power' is to prolong the process of decolonisation and give the imperialists time to strengthen their local allies and if possible to domesticate the nationalist leadership.

Nkrumah was well aware of what the colonial authorities were up to. He was determined not to become a harmless figurehead and fall into the trap set up by the colonialists. In March 1952, the Governor, Sir Arden-Clarke, announced that henceforth Nkrumah's title of 'Leader of Government Business' should be replaced by that of 'Prime Minister'. Many politicians would have been carried away by this honour, but Nkrumah kept his head. He understood that in a colonial framework an African prime minister would be restrained from fully promoting the interests of his people. It was for this reason that Nkrumah always emphasised the need for not losing sight of his movement's final goal. In December 1952 he wrote:

> Need we remind ourselves that the struggle is not over? The struggle still continues and intensifies as the end approaches. We have India, Ceylon and Burma to draw inspiration from.

Ours, therefore, at this hour of our struggle, is to keep on
organising and disciplining our forces for the final blow
against imperialism in our country, so as to make Ghana
take her rightful place among the community of
nations.[1]

Nkrumah argued that Ghana could not achieve freedom if it relied
merely on the good will and generosity of the colonial authorities.
He argued for a strategy of Tactical Action, based on vigilance and
pressure. It required the CPP to monitor carefully the activities of
the imperialists. At the same time pressure had to be exerted on the
colonial authorities so that positive steps were taken towards
decolonisation. Nkrumah argued that if this strategy was to be successful then the CPP had to maintain a high level of mobilisation. A
strong CPP enjoying popular support was the precondition for
allowing Nkrumah to retain the initiative.

Through the application of Tactical Action, Nkrumah was able
to push through a number of significant reforms. The Volta hydro-
electric project was initiated this way. Significant progress was
made in extending education. Improvements were made in housing
and health facilities. New roads, railways and bridges were constructed. Although far from satisfying the needs of the people, the
new projects represented a major gain for Ghana.

On 10 July 1953, Nkrumah decided to step up the pressure. On
that day, he moved a motion demanding independence in a speech
popularly known as the 'Motion of Destiny'. He told the Legislative
Assembly:

Mr Speaker, we have frequent examples to show that there
comes a time in the history of all colonial peoples when they
must, because of their will to throw off the hampering
shackles of colonialism, boldly assert their God-given right
to be free of a foreign ruler. Today we are here to claim this
right to our independence.[2]

The 'Motion of Destiny' placed independence firmly on the agenda.
Such a fundamental challenge to the existing constitution could not

1 *Freedom*, December 1952, no. 1.
2 Nkrumah, *Autobiography*, p. 157.

be pursued through the existing Legislative Assembly. A general election was organised to test the extent of support for Nkrumah. It was the colonial governor who insisted on the elections, but Nkrumah felt that such a test would only strengthen the case for independence.

Accordingly, all CPP brances in the 104 constituencies were placed on full alert. It was a hard-fought campaign and, as we shall argue later, it contained the seeds of the political conflict that was to haunt Ghana during the next two decades. However, the CPP came out of the election with its claim to represent the nation strengthened. It won 72 seats out of 104.

For the colonial authorities the results of the 1954 general elections still did not constitute a case for independence. Two years later, in 1956, they insisted on holding another general election. The results again confirmed the CPP's overwhelming popularity in the nation. Finally, after three election victories, Britain could no longer hold out against the inevitable. On 6 March 1957, Ghana became an independent African nation.

The Rise of the Opposition

Not everyone was happy with the progress of Nkrumah and the CPP. There was a group of Africans who had done well out of the colonial system and who feared that their special privileges would be threatened under independence. The educated African elite had a high opinion of itself and considered the rank-and-file supporters of the CPP to be nothing more than a rabble. Many of the chiefs appointed by the colonialists enjoyed considerable power and authority. Jealous of their position, they looked upon the CPP as a potential competitor. Although small in number, these individuals wielded considerable influence. They had education, wealth and prestige. Moreover, in any conflict, they could rely on their friends and contacts within the colonial officialdom.

The main difference between the supporters and opponents of the CPP was a special one. The strength of the CPP was among urban workers who had migrated to the towns in the previous decades. Ordinary peasants also responded to the CPP's message.

And young people in particular were solidly behind the CPP. The men of wealth and prestige had little in common with the masses. Their main concern was the defence and the extension of material privilege and not national independence. Since independence was perceived as a threat, it was inevitable that the elite would sooner or later come to oppose the very concept of nationhood itself. In opposition to national independence the elite celebrated regional autonomy and local interests. Thus the defence of material privilege in colonial Ghana was masked in the form of ethnicity and tribalism. By promoting regional ethnic values, the elite hoped to establish a local base for opposing the CPP and its strategy for national independence. In the pursuit of the anti-national approach the elite sought to take advantage of the system created by the colonial authorities. One of the key elements of the colonial policy in Ghana was the policy of divide and rule. Colonial officials had established a territorial system which fostered parochialism and regional consciousness. Each province and district was governed as a separate fiefdom which emphasised local as opposed to national interests. It was only in 1951 that the native authorities system was abolished and replaced by a system of elected local government. But local differences were encouraged by the colonial administration even after 1951, and the chiefs were warned that national centralisation would lead to their demise. Thus a system of local interests existed which could provide the opponents of the CPP with a cause and base of support.

The problem of anti-nationalist opposition first became manifest in the 1954 general election. In the lead up to the election a number of aspiring CPP candidates who were rejected by the local branches decided to run for office. Breaking with party discipline these candidates sought to promote their careers regardless of the consequences for the unity of the mass movement. Nkrumah reacted angrily to this attempt to split the ranks of the CPP an promptly had the renegade candidates expelled. Many of those expelled decided to secure their careers by joining a new party which had just been formed in the Northern territories called the Northern People's Party (NPP).

This was a significant development, for the NPP had no special reason for existence other than to represent regional interests. That it provided a haven for renegades from the CPP indicated the attraction which regional politics had for those whose main preoccupation was with their career. The NPP won 12 of the 21 Northern Territory seats. This was not much in comparison with the 72 seats won by the CPP, but it indicated that the threat of regional decisiveness could not be ignored.

The year 1954 represented an important turning point. At this stage the educated elite became aware of the opportunity for manipulating regional differences. An unholy alliance between the educated elite and the local tribal authorities began to take shape. No sooner were the elections over than the conservative African elite began to organise. The issue which they pushed to the fore was that of regional autonomy. They argued that the CPP's centralist organisation represented a danger to the local way of life. Many local chiefs resented Nkrumah's reform of local government and of the use of indirect councils. Anger at Nkrumah was particularly strong in Asante, where a powerful network of chiefs organised around a demand for a loose federation. It was this attempt to protect regional vested interest that led to the launching of the National Liberation Movement (NLM) in Kumasi in September 1954.

The NLM was launched with much traditional pomp and ceremony, with the support of the Asanteman Council of Chiefs. The NLM attempted to win popular support by agitating for higher cocoa prices for farmers. But its main concern was not the cocoa farmer but the preservation of the authority and influence of the chiefs. For the African elite, the NLM was a godsend. All the opponents of the CPP, such as Danquah, joined forces with the NLM. Blinded by naked ambition they were prepared to destroy the movement for national independence.

The opponents of the CPP had no inhibitions about promoting narrow tribalism. They would stop at nothing to prevent the emergence of an independent Ghana, run by a CPP government with the support of the masses. A statement submitted to the colonial authorities by the NLM and their allies indicates their reactionary intent:

> The peoples of these territories, belonging as they do to different tribes, have different structures of society, and are at different stages of adaptation and adoption of Western culture. . . . There is not enough consciousness of national identity to make possible easy and at the same time democratic unitary government. In the absence of this conscious-

ness, the safest course is to ensure that not all the powers of government are concentrated at the centre but that a substantial part of them is retained in the component territories where people have learned the habits and attitudes of living together for some time.[3]

Arguments which seek to postpone independence by claiming that African people have not yet adapted to 'Western culture' exemplify the mercenary spirit of the elite. A sophisticated defence of tribalism such as this only served to legitimate colonial rule. The NLM and its allies did everything to sabotage the efforts of Nkrumah and the CPP. Soon after its formation the NLM organised a campaign of violence designed to drive out the CPP from Asante. In 1955 this violence escalated and became a major threat to Nkrumah's strategy of achieving independence. That is why behind the scenes the colonialists were doing their best to support the NLM. Hence the murderer of Kofi Banda, a CPP protagonist shot dead at a rally at Ejitsu, was acquitted after he was brought to trial.

The anti-CPP provocations created a major dilemma for Nkrumah. The rank-and-file supporters of the CPP wanted to retaliate against the NLM. However, Nkrumah felt that if the CPP retaliated and a civil war broke out, the colonial authorities would use it as a pretext to intervene. Such a step would have led to the repression of the CPP and the scrapping of the Legislative Assembly. This was precisely what the imperialists did in British Guiana. There the colonial crack-down led to the mobilisation of the state apparatus against the forces of progress. Nkrumah was determined not to give the imperialists the excuse they were looking for. Later he recalled:

> My greatest difficulty at this time was to prevent Party members from hitting back. . . . I was not unsympathetic but I was convinced that severe discipline was the only thing that would assure our final victory. To strike back would have caused serious civil disturbances, probably even civil war, and they would have called for a state of emergency to be declared. This in turn would have invited intervention from Britain and, in the eyes of the whole world, there would be

3 Austen, *Politics in Ghana*, p. 277.

no doubt whatever that a country in a state bordering on civil war was hardly in a fit condition to take charge of its own affairs.[4]

Although the campaign of violence eventually subsided, the conservative tribalist elements managed to help postpone independence. The former Governor of India, Sir Frederic Bourne, was despatched to Ghana to work out a constitutional arrangement that would solve the political crisis. Moreover, the British argued that because of the conflict between the CPP and the NLM, another general election had to be held before independence could be granted. Even after the CPP's victory in the 1956 elections, the opposition did not give up. Dr Kofi Busia, one of the leaders of the opposition, even went to London to beg the colonialists not to give Ghana its independence. He told the British public: 'Sometimes I wonder why you are in such a hurry to leave us. Your experiment in the Gold Coast is not complete. We still need you – our country is not ready for parliament democracy.'[5]

Busia was absolutely clear where his loyalties lay. A servant of colonialism, he could not accept the victory of the progressive mass movement. Although he failed at the time to prevent the realisation of independence, Busia and his associates never lost hope that they could seize power from the people of Ghana.

The Dr Busias of this world demonstrated that there was in existence a group of prominent African politicians ready to stab the nationalist movement in the back. The emergence of this group indicated that independence would not be trouble-free. It showed that, despite the magnificent victories of the CPP, the imperialists had succeeded in building a bridgehead in Ghanaian society. That meant that even after the British left, their agents remained behind to act on their bidding.

The Dangers of Decolonisation

The emergence of conservative opposition during the phase of 'transfer of power' showed that decolonisation was not without its

4 Nkrumah, *Autobiography*, p. 181.
5 Ibid., p. 232.

dangers. But there were many others. The whole process of decolonisation was designed to move towards independence on terms dictated by the British. The main concern of the imperialists was to curb the radical influences and to educate nationalist leaders in the ways of their colonial masters. One of the greatest dangers facing Nkrumah was that as Prime Minister he would be held accountable for the running of a colonial system over which he had no control. The colonial authorities hoped that once in office Nkrumah would be forced to play by their rules and thus help to stabilise the situation. As the colonial authorities saw that situation, it was far easier to deal with a handful of nationalist politicians than with an unpredictable mass movement.

Nkrumah was not blind to the dangers posed by decolonisation. By accepting a role in the constitutional arrangement he risked becoming a pawn in the colonialists' game. To prevent this outcome, Nkrumah laid down strict guidelines on how CPP politicians should relate to the colonial system.

> There should be no fraternisation, I said, between Assembly-men and European officials except on strictly official relations: for what imperialists have failed to achieve by strong-arm methods, they might hope to bring off with cocktail parties. . . . To prove that we had not led this struggle for any personal aggrandisement, we had agreed that none of our party members in the Executive Council should go to live in the palatial ministerial bungalows that had been built for the purpose.
>
> Moreover, I continued, until such time as full self-government had been attained, I was strongly of the opinion that all Party members of the Assembly, as well as ministers, should surrender their salaries to the party and draw instead agreed remuneration from Party funds. This would prevent careerism and induce those in high office to live simply and modestly so as to maintain contact with the common people.[6]

These precautions were necessary to prevent the British from bribing individual representatives of the CPP and throwing the nationalist movement off course. By laying down a strict code of conduct the CPP managed to maintain its integrity and retained

6 Ibid., p. 117.

popular respect. For Nkrumah, the interlude of decolonisation was a frustrating one. The colonial officials were unwilling to give up their power. They did their best to wreck government policies initiated by Nkrumah. British civil servants through subterfuge attempted to delay the implementation of policy. The Chief Commissioners and the District Commissioners in the regions were particularly determined to slow down change. Behind the scenes they worked to undermine the authority of Nkrumah and his government.

The attitudes of the civil servants did not change even as Ghana approached the eve of independence. Symptomatic of this arrogance was the contemptuous way in which the British dealt with the issue of Ghana's constitution. The imperialists decided that it was their prerogative to decide the constitution of independent Ghana. Nkrumah's attempt to revise the proposed constitution in line with the needs of Ghana were out of hand rejected by the Secretary of State of the Colonial Office. The same attitude prevailed in relation to the organisation of the independence ceremonies. At first Nkrumah was informed that the ceremonies would be organised along the lines of those in Ceylon, to which Britain granted independence in 1948. But just a month before independence the Colonial Office changed its mind and decreed that the ceremonies would follow the example set by Australia's transfer to independence. When Nkrumah enquired to find out what the Australian example was, the Colonial Office indicated that it did not know. Then at the last moment, in the midst of considerable confusion, the Colonial Office decreed that Ghana would become independent following the Ceylon example. Even more insidious than the petty interference of the Colonial Office was the attempt of the security services to compromise Nkrumah and his comrades. The Special Branch never let up on its harassment of CPP activists. Nkrumah himself was kept under constant surveillance. Under these circumstances Nkrumah had always to be alert, for if he had made just one slip, the security services would have been only too happy to compromise him.

The most destructive element of the colonialists' strategy was its attempt to encourage opposition to Nkrumah and the CPP. The full story of the colonial authority's involvement with the NLM and the campaign of violence in Asante will probably never become public. But it was widely asserted that the NLM and the conservative

African politicians were not acting independently. As Nkrumah recalled:

> I could at one time almost guarantee that if there was any movement afoot against the Government, every attempt was made on the part of the civil service to enhance the opposition against the Government. Whether this was an example of the inherent sympathy of the British for the underdog is not clear, but it is liable to breed distrust.[7]

If anyone had any doubts, the inaction of the police and the army during the upsurge of violence in Asante showed where their sympathies lay.

The colonial authorities hoped that the conflict in Asante would get out of hand and that the ensuing instability would give them an opportunity to compromise and isolate Nkrumah. Back in Britain, the media took up the case of the opposition and blamed Nkrumah for the violence in Kumasi. Clearly, a propaganda drive was under way preparing public opinion for the eventual overthrow of Nkrumah. This was 1955. The British press had to wait eleven more years before their hopes were achieved.

In the end, the colonial regime could not subvert the struggle for independence by manipulating the opposition. But they did manage to inflict considerable damage on the people of Ghana. They had succeeded in sewing discord and dissension. By slowing down the pace of change they also won time to influence the terms on which decolonisation took place. And although the people were with Nkrumah, the state institutions remained the preserve of colonial influence. The civil service, the military, the police and the judiciary were very much the product of the colonial system. Not just the expatriates, but also the Africans who staffed these institutions looked at the world from the point of view of the old colonial system. Through these institutions and these individuals the colonial legacy could continue to influence an independent Ghana.

The opposition may have been defeated politically but the African elite had a monopoly of the special skills required to run the country. The colonialists had made sure that their African allies were well placed to exercise influence. Writing in 1968, Nkrumah recalled the problem that faced him on the eve of independence:

7 Ibid., p. 125.

> The first problem in Ghana at the time of independence was to make use of our pitifully small stock of professional and technical experts. Whatever their political views they had to be utilised to the full in the interest of the newly emerged Ghana State. From the start I had to bring not only into my cabinet but had to appoint to important posts in the judiciary, the civil service and the universities, individuals who had been active opponents of the Party in colonial days.[8]

Nkrumah had no choice but to utilise the skill and know-how of the small group of specialists trained during the colonial era. Yet it was precisely this group of Africans who had been the most active in the opposition and who had done so much to foster tribalism and regionalism. Looking back on the years 1951–7, it becomes evident that decolonisation did not mean merely the transition to independence. It also implied a parallel process through which the colonial authorities attempted to establish safeguards that could secure their objectives in the future. While Nkrumah worked towards the goal of independence, others laboured to make sure that independence would mean only a minimum of change. As the eve of independence approached, Nkrumah knew that one battle had been won but that the war would have to continue.

Preparing for Independence

Perhaps it all happened much too quickly. Nkrumah's ascendency as the leader of the nation occurred remarkably swiftly. With relatively little effort Nkrumah won the confidence of the masses and established the CPP as the organisational expression of the people's will. Such was his success that observers at the time were continually astounded by the speed of Nkrumah's progress. However, such speedy success was not without its problems. There were many obstacles on the way to independence; Ghana required practical solutions to a wide range of problems. It needed a unity of

8 Kwame Nkrumah, *Dark Days in Ghana*, London, Panaf Books, 1968, p. 65.

purpose, activists with skills necessary to run the nation and the commitment to see through the struggle to the bitter end.

Then Nkrumah faced an even more profound challenge. He had grasped from the outset the simple truth that political independence in itself did not constitute real independence. Ghana was not merely politically dominated by the colonialists. It was also economically controlled by Western interests. Unless Ghana succeeded in wresting control over its own economy, independence would be subverted and the people would be robbed of their birthright.Writing in October 1956, Nkrumah warned:

> The economic independence that should follow and maintain political independence demands every effort from the people, a total mobilisation of brain and manpower resources. What other countries have taken three hundred years or more to achieve, a once dependent territory must try to accomplish in a generation if it is to survive. Unless it is, as it were, 'jet-propelled', it will lag behind and thus risk everything for which it has fought.[9]

It was this recognition of the urgency of winning economic control over the country's resources that continually raised the question of whether the CPP and its supporters were ready for independence.

The challenge facing Nkrumah was a daunting one. Even at the most basic level there were difficulties. When Nkrumah became the leader of the Legislative Assembly there were virtually no Africans in responsible civil service positions. Lacking experience and qualifications, they could not be relied upon to run the essential services of the state. At the same time, British civil servants were resistant to the idea of training African personnel. The same problem was evident in the army, the police and the technical services. Nkrumah set about promoting the Africanisation of the civil service, but the risks were formidable. Unfortunately, the tasks facing the anticolonial movement were not merely technical ones. There were also major political problems that had to be confronted. Until 1951–2, Nkrumah and the CPP could devote virtually their entire energy to the goal of political independence. However, as Ghana moved closer to independence it became clear that the nation was

9 Nkrumah, *Autobiography*, p. vii.

far from united. Different interests, including opposition politicians and ethnic leaders, were pulling in different directions. Increasingly, Nkrumah was forced to devote as much time (if not more) to the issue of national unity as to the goal of national independence. Nkrumah was haunted by the threat of disunity. If the African masses were divided then all the plans for independence could be wrecked. Consequently, Nkrumah decided to pursue the strategy of compromise and to try to forge the broadest support possible for the struggle for national independence. Inevitably this meant that important interest groups who were primarily concerned with their own narrow privileges, such as the colonial chiefs, were able to retain considerable influence.

As Prime Minister Nkrumah's energies were also taken up with the practical problems of running the colonial government. Such a responsibility necessarily limited the time he had available for the organisation and supervision of the CPP. This was probably the greatest problem facing Nkrumah. At the end of the day the CPP was the only instrument that the masses could rely on to defend their interests.It was only the CPP that could provide organisation and direction to the people. Unlike other institutions, the CPP was the people's own creation. It was an organ through which popular will could be mobilised for the construction of the nation. But for that to occur the CPP itself had to be prepared for the challenges facing an independent Ghana.

To prepare the CPP for its responsibilities in such difficult circumstances would require the full-time leadership of Nkrumah. The organisation of the party had to be strengthened and its activists educated and trained. *It is one of the tragedies of this period that Nkrumah could not devote the time and energy that the qualitative transformation of the CPP required. Of course Nkrumah did what he could. But without his constant presence and attention the CPP failed to make a transition from a mass political party to a movement that could provide leadership and win authority in every aspect of social life.*

Nkrumah did not deceive himself about the failure of the CPP to prepare itself for independence. It was obvious to him that there was not enough time to create a party membership with the vision and ideology required for the creation of a new nationhood. Later in 1961, Nkrumah explained this problem to the CPP Study Group in Accra in the following way: 'We cannot build Socialism without

Socialists and we must take positive steps to ensure that the Party and the country produce the men and the women who can handle a Socialist Programme.'

The CPP lacked the education that a progressive party requires to change the world. Unfortunately, the party also lacked the coherence that was essential to realise its mission. During the years leading up to independence the CPP would not remain the preserve of the highly committed anti-colonial activists. To strengthen the spirit of national unity the party attempted to broaden its base of support. Nkrumah and other leaders of the CPP hoped that the new supporters would quickly become influenced by the party's ideals. However, many individuals joined to further their careers. Nkrumah understood that these people could erode the integrity of the party but at the same time felt that Ghana needed their skills and expertise. Later, in 1968, he reflected on this problem and characterised it as a 'calculated risk'.

In a similar vein Nkrumah felt that the CPP could not simply ignore the pressure emanating from the regionalist quarters. Indeed, some of the parochial sentiments on which regionalism thrived actually acquired influence inside the CPP. Nkrumah noted:

> I had to combat not only tribalism but the African tradition that a man's first duty was to his family group and that therefore nepotism was the highest of all virtues. While I believe we had largely eliminated tribalism as an active force, its by-products and those of the family system were still with us. I could not have chosen my government without some regard to tribal origins, and even, within the Party itself, there was at times a tendency to condemn or recommend some individual on the basis of his tribal or family origin.[10]

Obviously, a new party like the CPP could not remain immune to the old values that prevailed in the country. That these values existed within the party was inevitable. It also indicated that the CPP had to be taken through a thoroughgoing process of training and education. Today, the intelligent reader can see that the CPP and the broader movement were not ready for independence. But

10 Nkrumah, *Dark Days in Ghana*, p. 66.

what else could Nkrumah and the CPP have done? The obstacles facing the anti-colonial movement were formidable. It was not possible to rid the country of colonial influences overnight, and unpleasant decisions had to be made in the interests of the goal of independence. In a sense, the recognition that the CPP was not prepared for independence is a platitude. History never waits for individuals until they are ready but forces humanity to make decisions there and then. What often separates those who make history from those who do not is the willingness to take the risks and jump before they are ready.

Nkrumah had no choice but to act as he did. He did not have the luxury of time. Had he slowed down the movement for change, the colonialists would have had more time to interfere through the process of decolonisation. They would have been more able to exploit divisions in the nationalist movement and perhaps even to strengthen the hands of the conservative opposition. For in the end preparation was not a question of time but the ability to act, free of the constraints of the colonial system. For Nkrumah, this period of transition represented a mixture of glory and pain. In a race against time many problems had remained unsolved. But Ghana was independent. Against all the odds, Nkrumah had guided the nation to the threshold of its destiny.

Chapter 6

On Borrowed Time

Ghana entered the era of independence with so much to be done. Nkrumah was under no illusions about the trials ahead. The old colonial powers had not conceded defeat; they had merely changed their tactics. They had not given up their attempt to control Ghana. Their objective was to retain influence by indirect means. To that end they left behind a country which lacked the means to prosper on its own. Ghana's colonial economy was designed to serve the interests of the world market. It was an economy artificially imposed on the country, an economy indifferent to the real needs of the indigenous population. During the colonial period, Ghana was reorganised to become an appendage of Europe. Ghana's wealth flowed outwards and the nation was deprived of the resources necessary for modernisation and development.

The colonial state and its various institutions were created to oversee Ghana's economic enslavement. The civil servants and other state employees were carefully educated and trained by the British. They were left behind as the local representatives of the colonial power – men who could be relied upon to preserve the colonial way of life even after independence. The British-trained middle class had no interest in change. They were the beneficiaries of the colonial system and, as far as they were concerned, any real change would be more of a threat to them than to their foreign masters.

From the outset at independence, the middle class and a small group of capitalists devoted their energy to preserving the old colonial way of life. Within months after independence, this group, now organised under the banner of the United Party (UP), was plotting against the Nkrumah government. And the Western press, particularly the British media, were more than happy to adopt the UP's cause as their own. By 1958 the British *Daily Telegraph* was denouncing the Nkrumah government as 'a corrupt, cruel and vulgar tyranny'. This alliance between Western interests and local agents acted as a permanent threat to Ghana's sovereignty.

Nkrumah certainly controlled the government, but the government did not control the state. The forces of colonisation were carefully concentrated around the machinery of the state. The British had paid considerable attention to the police and the army. Although there were many loyal Ghanaians inside the military, among the officer corps pro-British elements predominated. Many of the officers trained in Britain had adopted the elitist arrogance of the colonial military caste. They mixed in a select circle of well-to-do businessmen and top civil servants. Their loyalty was very much attached to this circle and not to the nation they were intended to serve. This powerful section of Ghanaian society presented Nkrumah with a dilemma. As he wrote in 1968:

> I could have dismissed many of the higher police officers about whose loyalty I had doubts. But whom could I have put in their place? So little education was done in colonial times that actual illiteracy was a major problem in the army and the police.[1]

The same question posed by Nkrumah could be related time and time again to all the colonial institutions. These were all unreliable instruments for the purpose of nation building. But what could Nkrumah 'put in their place'? Under such difficult circumstances Nkrumah chose the economy as the field of battle where the struggle for independence would be fought. For Nkrumah understood that a nation that could not control its own resources and the use to which they were put could never be free.

1 Nkrumah, *Dark Days in Ghana*, p. 66.

The Battle Against Underdevelopment

Nkrumah argued that the economy inherited by independent Ghana constituted the main threat to the future of the nation. He wrote on this subject:

> We had to work fast. Under colonial rule, foreign monopoly interests had tied up our whole economy to suit themselves. We had not a single industry. Our economy was dependent on one cash crop – cocoa. Although our output of cocoa is the largest in the world, there was not one single cocoa processing factory.[2]

Like other colonies in the Third World, Ghana was underdeveloped. Economic life was distorted to serve the interest of the colonial powers, and a situation was created which made it impossible for Ghana to function as a viable economic unit. Ghana was forced to become a producer of cocoa. There is nothing objectionable about producing cocoa. But when the economy of a nation is concentrated around the production of a single commodity, then inevitable problems arise. It means that the economic future of a country is dependent on forces entirely out of its control. The demand for cocoa is dependent on the consumption levels of a handful of Western nations. Changes in demand lead to fluctuations in prices, with devastating consequences for the producer nation concerned.

That Ghana was forced to organise its economy around one crop was bad enough. To make matters worse, the people of Ghana had little control over the one crop on which so much was staked. Africans produced cocoa and the European trade firms marketed it. The marketing of cocoa was monopolised by Europeans who were able to use their position to determine the price paid to the producers. In this way, they were able to make high profits without incurring any risks. The African producer of cocoa was left with very little after the European marketing firms and the colonial taxmen were through with him. It has been estimated that the African producer usually ended up with less than a third of the revenues

2 Ibid., p. 76.

obtained from cocoa production.

The colonial economy was organised around the needs of European interests. The only good roads that existed were ones built for the European-owned gold mines and timber industries. Before Nkrumah came to office in 1951, there was no direct railway access between Accra and Takoradi, the main port of the period. Passengers had to make their way via Kumasi, which was the centre of the timber and mining industries. The revenues from cocoa were invested in British banks instead of promoting local industry. Even the most obvious forms of investment (such as in the processing of cocoa) were ignored by the colonial authorities.

The refusal to invest in industry made sense from the British point of view. Ghana became a market for British goods. Local industry would have been only an obstacle to this profitable trade. Resources that could have assisted the industrialisation of Ghana were then squandered to pay for British imports of non-durable consumer goods. The lack of an industrial base was shown by one striking fact: when the CPP first came to power in 1951, there were in existence only 104 small-scale industrial establishments throughout the whole of Ghana.

Nkrumah realised that 104 small industrial establishments could not provide the foundations for economic development and industrialisation. To develop, Ghana needed to diversify its economy to areas other than cocoa and to introduce new techniques of production. During the early years of independence, Nkrumah concentrated on expanding the infrastructure of the nation to provide a springboard for industrialisation. A network of new roads were constructed, a new harbour was opened in Tema, and plans were established for the completion of new industrial plants. In the meantime resources were devoted to the completion of the great Volta River Dam project. Revenues were also made available for the diversification and mechanisation of agriculture. The Nkrumah government also placed a great emphasis on investing in social services. State recurrent expenditure increased about four times between 1951 and 1960. Nkrumah took the radical step of making all education free. And a mass literacy campaign made Ghana the most literate nation in Africa. Similar achievements were made in health care, and infant mortality decreased thanks to the newly established network of maternity and post-natal care centres.

Until 1961 Nkrumah did little to challenge the colonial economic system. He used the years 1957–61 to consolidate his regime and to establish the infrastructure for future industrialisation. After 1961 the struggle to transform the economy could no longer be avoided. As an economy orientated towards an open market, Ghana continued to rely on the importation of foreign goods. Resources required for investment in industry were frittered away on imports of consumer goods. There were no advantages to remaining an open economy. The expected flow of capital from Western nations never materialised, and Ghana had no option but to devise a strategy based on economic self-sufficiency. Worse still, the price of cocoa on the world market continued to fall. Through improvements in agriculture the production of cocoa was on the increase. But it seemed that the more cocoa Ghana produced, the less it was worth. The price of cocoa, which was $850 per ton in 1957, had dropped to $490 in 1961. Clearly, Ghana could not continue in the old way.

In 1961 steps were taken to move Ghana towards a socialist transformation of its economy. The new approach was codified in the CPP's new programme for Work and Happiness adopted in 1962. Reflecting the background to the adoption of this programme, Nkrumah wrote:

> Immediately after Independence, while wishing to proceed on a socialist path of economic and social development, it was considered advisable, in view of the circumstances operating at the time, to pursue a 'shopping list' approach, estimating how much we could afford, and allocating it to projects drawn up into a list according to priority. But it soon became clear that this approach was not producing results quickly enough, and it was to speed up our socialist programme by comprehensive economic plans which would utilise all the economic and extra-economic resources of the nation. . . . It would not have been possible, given the political and economic conditions of the pre-1960 period, to have embarked on full-scale socialist programmes earlier. Bourgeois economic interests were too entrenched to be removed entirely, or overnight. Ghana inherited at Independence almost total trade dependence on the West. Our economy was almost completely foreign or local capitalist owned.[3]

3 Kwame Nkrumah, *Revolutionary Path*, p. 181–2.

So, according to Nkrumah, it took three years after independence before Ghana could embark on a strategy of socialist development. It was the recognition that three precious years had been lost that forced Nkrumah to change gears in a dash for growth with the programme for Work and Happiness.

The ideas behind the new economic strategy were straightforward. The continual declining price of cocoa on the world market had shown that Ghana could not get by on the revenues made from a single crop. Ghana had to industrialise fast before those revenues declined further. Since the indigenous class of capitalists was very weak, the only instrument available for industrialisation was the state. For this reason the new economic strategy gave pride of place to state enterprise. The Seven-Year Development Plan launched in March 1964 envisaged that industrialisation would proceed through enterprises owned by the state or jointly owned by the state and private enterprise or foreign investors. One of the aims of the plan was to encourage co-operatives and to discourage the consolidation of an indigenous capitalist class. Another objective of the plan was to assume greater state control over trade to ensure that precious resources were not spent on foreign consumer and luxury goods. In fact the new economic strategy still represented a compromise. Nkrumah recognised that Ghana was still not free to pursue a socialist economic strategy. Ghana was still heavily reliant on foreign finance. Projects such as the Volta River Dam required external finance for their completion. If Ghana had embarked on a total socialist strategy, then the country would have faced the wrath of Western business. In order to minimise the effects of Western hostility, Nkrumah pursued a gradualist programme for change – one that was based on the steady encroachment of the state sector on the economy. Nkrumah justified this approach thus:

> The strategy was for the public sector, which controlled key areas of the economy, gradually to overtake the private sector until eventually the private sector was entirely eliminated. During this phasing-out period, joint projects involving state and private enterprise were embarked upon. It was considered, in the circumstances, that the undertaking of joint projects with already operating capitalist concerns was better than the alternative of economic blockade by the

west and consequent lack of development until the assistance of socialist states could be procured and become operational.[4]

The implementation of such a compromise strategy necessarily raised key problems. A radical st.ategy inevitably threatens the indigenous pro-colonial forces and their allies abroad. At the same time, if pursued in a gradual fashion it only threatens them in the long run. This gives time to the pro-capitalist forces to organise against the anti-colonial movement. Nkrumah recognised that this was a problem he had to live with.

Another obstacle in the way of the successful implementation of Work and Happiness was the need for the people to make sacrifices in the interest of the nation. Before living standards could be raised a new economy had to be constructed. This required large investments and the curbing of consumption. In 1961 an austerity budget was introduced to ensure that resources were concentrated towards the objective of industrialisation. The hardships that austerity imposes on ordinary people always contain the potential for mass discontent and conflict. Only if the government and the ruling party are sensitive to the mood of the people can problems be avoided. In his dash for growth Nkrumah understood that he had little time. He had to demonstrate to the nation that his strategy would yield results and that sacrifices made by the people would soon bring them their reward.

Finally, Nkrumah's economic strategy faced a hurdle even more insurmountable than most. Ghana, like other African nations, was an artificial creation of imperialism. Although well-endowed with natural resources, Ghana lacked the size necessary for a viable long-term developmental strategy. Nkrumah was a fervent Pan-Africanist not because he was a pious dreamer but because he recognised the realities of the situation. Divided into individual nations, Africa could not prosper. African countries on their own lacked the strength to withstand Western interests. Only if Africa functioned as one large economic unit could it develop into a modern industrialised continent. This was a theme to which Nkrumah returned time and time again:

4 Ibid., p. 182.

The other major problem facing development, the really crucial one, was the problem of economic scale. Ghana, like the majority of independent African states, is too small an economic unit in terms of population and resources. The optimum zone of development for the African people is the entire continent of Africa. Until there is an All-African Union Government pursuing socialist policies, and planning the economic development of Africa as a whole, the standard of living of the African masses will remain low, and they will continue to suffer from neo-colonial exploitation and the oppression of the indigenous bourgeoisie.[5]

Nkrumah's contribution to Pan-Africanism will be explored in the next chapter. Suffice it to say that for Nkrumah it was a life-and-death issue on which the economic development of Ghana depended.

It was with the recognition of important obstacles to Ghana's socialist development that Nkrumah introduced the Seven-Year Development Plan to the National Assembly. In the light of subsequent events it is worth recalling his motivation for the plan:

We are determined that the economic independence of Ghana shall be achieved and maintained so as to avoid the social antagonisms resulting from the unequal distribution of economic power. We are equally determined to ensure that the operation of a mixed economy leads to the socialist transformation we envisage, and not to the defeat of our socialist aims. It is essential, therefore, that we should remind ourselves at all times of the necessity firstly to promote to the maximum the development of the state and cooperative sectors; secondly to regulate the pattern of state investment in order to give the highest priority to productive investment, and thirdly to determine and direct the forms and conditions of foreign investment, in order to safeguard our socialist policy and national independence.[6]

This was the outlook that influenced Ghana's economic policy

5 Ibid., p. 183.
6 Ibid., p. 191.

during the years leading up to 1966.

Whatever the shortcomings of Nkrumah's strategy, the results were impressive. The Volta River project brought Ghana into the industrial age. It provided the foundation for an industrial complex for the future. Important state enterprises were established in other sectors. The state invested in oil and sugar refineries, meat-canning, soap- and paint-making factories, and a vehicle-assembly plant. Investments were also directed towards agro-related industries so as to provide the foundation for meat-canning and sugar production. Other initiatives in this sector were designed to lower Ghana's dependence on food imports such as meat, rice and sugar. As a result of these policies, Ghana's real gross national product increased by 24.5 per cent between 1960 and 1965. Although Ghana still had a long way to travel, the new enterprises established during this period provided the country with a new structural foundation for economic growth. And this occurred despite the dramatic decline in the price of cocoa during the years 1960 to 1965.

The Reality of Imperialism

Imperialism did not give Nkrumah much time. As soon as Nkrumah embarked on his strategy of socialist economic development he became a marked man. As far as imperialism was concerned it made no difference that Nkrumah was prepared to compromise. Any challenge to imperialist interests had to be crushed lest it should serve as an example to other Third World countries. If Nkrumah was ready to crawl he would be left alone. But if he chose to defy Western business then Ghana would face economic war. The shift in attitude towards Nkrumah coincides with his government's policy initiatives in 1961.

In 1961, loans and forms of credit from the West began to dry up. A campaign of slander directed against Ghana in the Western press set the tone for the next five years. In September 1961, the *New York Times* suggested that Washington might hold back its promised aid for the Volta River project. It reported that President Kennedy wanted 'reassurances on the political orientation of the Nkrumah Government'.[7] A week later this newspaper returned to

7 *New York Times,* 23 Sept. 1961.

the subject, and reported that 'the United States Administration sources expressed concern today over indications that Ghana was inclining more and more toward a pro-Soviet position in foreign affairs and a Marxist dictatorship at home'.[8] What Washington found offensive was that the Nkrumah government had taken some long-overdue steps to rid the country of its colonial influence. One such 'Marxist' step was the replacement of the British Major-General Alexander, who was serving as Chief-of-Staff of the army, by a Ghanaian officer. The other was a cabinet shake-up, which saw the resignation of ministers closely linked to capitalist interests.

Washington had no inhibitions about interfering in Ghana's internal affairs. During the next two months press reports continued to portray Ghana as on the edge of disaster due to the irrational policies of the Nkrumah government. In the end, President Kennedy agreed to honour his previous undertaking to provide credit for the construction of the Volta River project. But the loan was now to be provided in stages 'so that any sharp deviation in President Nkrumah's political and fiscal course could be dealt with before all the funds are spent'.[9] In other words, Washington's loan was conditional on Nkrumah not going too far and too fast in the implementation of his economic programme.

Although Ghana got the loan necessary for the completion of the Volta River project, the campaign of slander orchestrated through the Western press was beginning to have its effect. It became increasingly difficult for Ghana to obtain long-term credit from Western sources. Ghana was forced to rely on expensive short-term and middle-term credit, which created major problems for the country's financial position. The invisible war conducted by the Western banks placed Ghana in an intolerable position. Without access to credit, Ghana could not maintain the momentum of its high rate of growth. Soon industry in Ghana began to suffer from shortages of raw materials and spare parts for machinery.

But there was worse to come. If the blockade on credit did not bring Ghana to its knees, then imperialism had plenty of other means in reserve. Unfortunately for Ghana, the Western powers still controlled the world-wide marketing of cocoa and could set the price for this commodity. In the mid-sixties, the imperialists

8 *New York Times*, 30 Sept. 1961.
9 *New York Times*, 16 Dec. 1961.

stepped up their campaign against Ghana and purposely pushed down the price of cocoa. In 1965 the price of cocoa was driven so low that it was hardly worth producing it. Britain and the USA had deliberately engineered a situation that could only have a catastrophic impact on Ghana's economy. It is of course now a matter of public record that imperialism did not restrict its aggression to the economic sphere. Its economic war against Nkrumah was only a prelude to political intervention. Once the economy was destabilised, the local agents of imperialism were organised to put an end to the Nkrumah era in Ghana. And once Western objectives were achieved, the price of cocoa began to rise 'miraculously' on the world market. All of a sudden credit and foreign aid began to flow into Ghana. For imperialism now faced in Ghana a government with which it could do business.

The Dilemma of Power

The struggle for economic independence could not be waged by economic measures alone. Nkrumah had always recognised that the ultimate guarantee of Ghana's future was a party with strong roots in the masses. Without popular support Nkrumah had little chance against foreign pressures. Nor could Nkrumah hope to implant his plans for a socialist transformation of Ghana if he did not enjoy the confidence of his people. Speaking to a CPP rally in 1960, Nkrumah emphasised the need to win popular support for radical economic policies and an acceptance of the hardships that such policies implied in the short term. He warned:

> We have won the political battle and have now plunged ourselves into the fight for economic and social reconstruction of our country.... This fight is tougher and far more difficult than many of us realise....
>
> Furthermore we must realise that even many of our comrades, dedicated patriots who are devoted to the Party cause, would hesitate to fight on our side in this battle for economic freedom and reconstruction, because they do not understand the nature of our struggle.[10]

10 Nkrumah, 'Speech on 10th Anniversary of Positive Action', in *Selected Speeches of Dr Kwame Nkrumah*, Vol. 1, Ghana, Affram Publications, 1961, p. 4.

Nkrumah's comments were prescient and to the point. In September 1961 strikes broke out in the country, indicating that the CPP had much to do if it was to continue to enjoy the support of the people.

Looking back on the crucial years 1960–6, it appears that the transformation of the CPP into a living mass movement was not completed. At the time appearances were deceptive. Popular support for Nkrumah ensured that the right-wing opposition groups were always held in check. The middle classes and the local capitalists lacked the support necessary for taking on Nkrumah. So what went wrong? In an interesting recollection of the period, Nkrumah himself gives the answer to our question:

> We expected opposition to our development plans from the relics of the old 'opposition', from the Anglophile intellectual and professional elite, and of course from neo-colonialists who viewed the obvious signs of our approaching independence with growing alarm. What we did not perhaps anticipate sufficiently was the backsliding of some of our own Party members, men like Gbedemah and Adamafio, who for reasons of personal ambition, and because they only paid lip service to socialism, sought to destroy the Party.[11]

It is a testimony to Nkrumah's integrity that he locates the source of the downfall of his experiment inside the CPP.

The problem of mass organisation and party building was always at the forefront of Nkrumah's thought. As he noted on numerous occasions, 'socialism cannot be built without socialists'. It was for this reason that Nkrumah always advocated the necessity for education and political training. The Kwame Nkrumah Ideological Institute at Winneba, established in 1962, was designed precisely to educate the CPP activists in socialist theory. Unfortunately, by the time this education was beginning to have its effect, it was too late.

At this stage, it is worth exploring the difficulties faced by the CPP in educating itself to become a socialist party. According to Nkrumah, the CPP suffered from its role as a broad-base movement. At first sight this sounds ironic, for it was precisely its broad-based support that allowed the CPP to play a leading role in the

11 Nkrumah, *Dark Days in Ghana*, p. 68.

anti-colonial struggle. To understand Nkrumah's point of view it is necessary to make a distinction between a movement that is itself broad-based and a movement that enjoys mass support. If the movement itself is broad-based, it loses its ability to act decisively. Instead of leading the nation, the movement becomes merely a reflection of the different sections of society. Such a movement can make headway during the phase of the anti-colonial struggle, but it becomes ineffective in the post-independence period when advance requires the radical transformation of society.

Nkrumah has explained this point well in his argument for the creation of a 'well-disciplined progressive party pursuing revolutionary policies'. He noted:

> The broad base on which it was necessary to construct the party while the struggle for national liberation was being waged, meant that it contained many who had strong reservations about the kind of society they wished to see constructed after independence. Indigenous bourgeois and petty bourgeois elements, deeply committed to capitalism, aspired to replace the foreigner and not to see power pass to the masses. . . . After independence, therefore, party organisation and discipline must be tightened and strengthened, and ideological education of the masses pursued with the utmost rigour.[12]

According to Nkrumah, ideological differences between different sections of society were evident inside the CPP but could not be brought out into the open until independence was achieved. However, once the 'political revolution' had been won, the party could move towards transforming itself into a radical revolutionary force.

On the intellectual level, Nkrumah had a fine appreciation of party organisation. However, a number of difficulties arose inside the CPP which could not be anticipated intellectually. With ideological issues inside the CPP remaining unresolved before independence, the question of what views would prevail after independence was left open. Without a carefully organised ideological campaign, even reactionary views could gain a foothold inside the party. Indeed, the dangers were even greater once independence was won. After independence, the CPP became the party of the state.

12 Nkrumah, *Revolutionary Path*, pp. 151–2.

As such, it became one of the most important institutions in the nation. Naturally, everyone interested in acquiring power and influence joined the party. The most dubious careerists signed up to gain influence and material advantage. Under such circumstances it is not surprising that the CPP itself became influenced by the self-seeking, power-hungry politicians who were only involved for material gain. The corrosive influence of these elements on party life became increasingly evident. There were growing signs that party membership ceased to have any political meaning: it had become a meal ticket.

Many CPP officials abused their position of trust to reap material benefits. Even ministers were involved in dubious deals and encouraged the taking of bribes. As corruption inside the CPP grew, Nkrumah decided to act. In April 1961, Nkrumah made his dramatic Dawn Broadcast: 'it was a call to action to revitalise the CPP, to end self-seeking, to energise the efforts of the people towards socialism; in short, to stir up the people to fight the battle of the mind with greater determination'.[13] The Dawn Broadcast denounced corruption both inside and outside the CPP. It laid down the law and declared war against corruption in high places. As a statement of political standards expected of progressive militants, the Dawn Broadcast retains its relevance to this day. It also contains important insights into the correct relationship between the party and the masses.

> It is most important to remember that the strength of the Convention People's Party derives from the masses of the people. These men and women include those whom I have constantly referred to as the unknown warriors – dedicated men and women who serve the party loyally and selflessly without hoping for reward. It is therefore natural for the masses to feel some resentment when they see comrades whom they have put into power and given the mandate to serve the country on their behalf, begin to forget themselves and indulge in ostentatious living. . . . Some of us very easily forget that we ourselves have risen from among the masses. We must avoid any conduct that will breed antagonism and uneasy relations.[14]

13 Ibid., p. 93.
14 Ibid., p. 150.

It is significant that the Dawn Broadcast was made to the people of Ghana as a whole and not just to the membership of the CPP. In a sense Nkrumah was calling on the masses to help revitalise the CPP. In taking such an unprecedented step Nkrumah gave a signal that at the end of the day he had more confidence in the people than in his own party.

Corruption did not only undermine the effectiveness of the CPP; it also created suspicion and mistrust between the people and the governing party. History has shown that, once a party loses the trust of the masses, it finds it difficult to win it back. It is very much a proof of Nkrumah's greatness that, despite the stagnation of the CPP, his leadership of the nation continued to enjoy popular support. The CPP may have lost touch with its mass base, but Nkrumah retained the affection and support of ordinary people. In the end it was Nkrumah's own party that ensured his downfall. The selfish, arrogant CPP officers who scoffed at the party's ideals helped paralyse the only institution that could have guaranteed popular power. Without a mass progressive party, not even Nkrumah could withstand the forces of imperialism inside and outside Ghana.

Like all great men in history Nkrumah played for high stakes. Nothing but the best was good enough for his people, and he was not prepared to exchange Ghana's destiny for a few crumbs from the table of imperialism. Nkrumah pursued this course because he recognised that Ghana had no choice. For Ghana, socialism was not an option but the only policy that could secure a future for the nation. But Nkrumah was living on borrowed time. He had built a new world with few resources at his disposal. And all that time he knew that his work was always subject to the sabotage of imperialist interests. In the end the obstacles proved insurmountable – not because Nkrumah's objectives were hopelessly unrealistic but because there were not enough people trained to fight the new enemy. Too often Nkrumah fought as a solitary figure without an army. His army, the CPP, simply remained behind the times. In the end Nkrumah was defeated. However, Ghana has much to learn from Nkrumah's defeat. For the Nkrumah experiment still needs to be completed, but this time defended by an army of cadres that is trained, educated and totally committed to the future of the nation.

Chapter 7

Giving Reality to the Pan-African Ideal

Despite the demise of his experiment in Ghana, Nkrumah as leader, thinker and activist continues to inspire a new generation of Africans. Nkrumah continues to influence political discourse not just in Ghana but throughout Africa and the black diaspora. There are many reasons why Nkrumah's ideas still retain such influence over contemporary political discussions. But without any doubt it is Nkrumah's contribution to the development and popularisation of Pan-Africanism that explains his present-day relevance.

Pan-Africanism as an ideal did not originate with Nkrumah. But it is only with Nkrumah that Pan-Africanism ceased to be a dream and became a practical possibility. Until Nkrumah, Pan-Africanism had had the character of a worthwhile ideal. Pan-Africanists such as DuBois and Padmore advocated African unity as a political response to racial oppression and colonial domination. In their hands, Pan-Africanism developed into a coherent ideological perspective. Since they were removed by circumstance from involvement in mass politics they were not able to take Pan-Africanism beyond an ideology and give it a practical and organisational shape. It is only with Nkrumah that Pan-Africanism ceases to be merely ideology and acquires the dimension of practical action.

From the outset of his involvement in mass politics Nkrumah recognised that the future development of Ghana and of Africa as a whole were inextricably linked. Time and again Nkrumah argued that the geographical territories created during the colonial era could not prosper as independent entities. As Nkrumah saw it, the carving up of Africa by the imperialists had led to the creation of artificial statelets. The very artificiality of such nations was in the interests of the imperialists, who could continue to dominate their creations even after the colonial era. He noted:

> The intention is to use the new African states, so circum-
> scribed, as puppets through whom influence can be
> extended. . . . The creation of several weak and unstable
> states of this kind in Africa, it is hoped, will ensure the con-
> tinued dependence on the former colonial powers for
> economic aid, and impede African unity. This policy of
> balkanisation is the new imperialism, the new danger to
> Africa.[1]

The danger of the Balkanisation of Africa haunted Nkrumah during his politically active years. An Africa divided along the boundaries of the colonial era could not withstand the external forces that preyed upon it. The colonial domination of Africa was, and remains, a convenience for the imperialists. It creates a con-tinent easily prey to foreign domination.

According to Nkrumah, an Africa of separate nation states would be divided up into distinct spheres of influence by foreign powers. African nations would end up having closer links with foreign power blocs than with other African nations. He wrote:

> While we in Africa, for whom the goal of unity is paramount,
> are striving in this direction, the neo-colonialists are straining
> every nerve to upset it by encouraging the formation of com-
> munities based on the language of their former colonisers.
> We cannot allow ourselves to be so disorganised and
> divided. The fact that I speak English does not make me an
> Englishman. Similarly, the fact that some of us speak French
> or Portuguese does not make us Frenchmen or Portuguese.
> We are Africans first and last, and as Africans our best inter-
> ests can only be served by uniting within an African Com-
> munity. Neither the Commonwealth nor a Franco-African
> Community can be a substitute.[2]

1 Nkrumah, *Africa Must Unite*, p. 179.
2 Nkrumah, *Revolutionary Path*, p. 223.

Regional blocs provide a framework for imperialist domination. As Nkrumah accurately anticipated, they represent a new mechanism for partitioning Africa. This can be seen most vividly in the case of Francophone Africa, whose member states remain semi-colonies of France. Nkrumah held that the Balkanisation of Africa not only meant foreign domination but also invited tension and conflict between the people of the continent. Artificial boundaries necessarily breed suspicion and tension, providing the foundation for perpetual conflict among Africans. In a speech delivered at the summit conference of the Organisation of African Unity [OAU] in July 1964, Nkrumah stated:

> Serious border disputes have broken out and disturbed our Continent since our last meeting. Fortunately, good sense and African solidarity have prevailed in all these instances. But the disputes have been smothered, not settled. The artificial divisions of African States are too numerous and irrational for real permanent and harmonious settlements to be reached, except within the framework of a Continental union.
>
> How, for example, can we prevent the people of Western Somalia, whose livelihood is cattle grazing, from continuing to look for fresh fields for grazing by travelling beyond traditional barriers without bringing them into clashes with their compatriots in Ethiopia?[3]

Hence Balkanisation also meant permanent strife within Africa. A geographical division which did not correspond to real historical development would necessarily fuel conflict and wars. Such a political map represented permanent instability for the people of Africa.

Nkrumah also portrayed Balkanisation as an instrument that facilitated Africa's economic enslavement. While foreign capital operated a continent-wide strategy, Africans could only draw on the resources of a single nation. This was an unequal contest, since foreign capital could move from region to region while the local African economy was entirely dependent on foreign capital. As Nkrumah explains:

3 Ibid., pp. 281–2.

> In Africa, most of the independent states are economically
> unviable, and still have the artificial frontiers of colonialism.
> They are easy prey for the voracious appetites of neo-
> colonialist empire-builders. Where political Balkanisation
> has not been successful for the imperialists, economic
> Balkanisation has been pursued. A single productive process
> is divided between states. . . . The regional economic group-
> ings in Africa have been encouraged, controlled by neo-
> colonialists, which therefore further strengthen international
> finance capital.[4]

From his grasp of the dangers presented by the Balkanisation of the
continent, Nkrumah concluded that the struggle for freedom could
only be conducted from a Pan-Africanist perspective. As a collection of artificially created states, Africa is doomed to stagnation and
poverty. Accordingly, Pan-African unity is not a policy option but a
question of survival. Only a continent-wide division of labour can
create the conditions for the qualitative transformation of life.

Nkrumah understood that independence could not mean very
much in economic terms within the context of an isolated African
nation. He remarked: 'No independent African State today has a
chance to follow an independent course of economic development
by itself, and many of us who have tried to do this have been almost
ruined or have had to return to the fold of the former colonial
rulers.'[5] It was this understanding that made Nkrumah determined
to practise a Pan-Africanist policy from the first day of Ghana's
independence.

Pan-Africanism in Practice

As long as Nkrumah only talked about Pan-Africanism few
objected. Indeed, virtually every African leader pays lip-service to
the Pan-Africanist ideal. However, once Nkrumah indicated that
he intended to act and not just talk, opposition began to mount.

4 Ibid., p. 313.
5 Ibid.

Many African leaders and politicians both inside and outside Ghana had developed strong interests in the perpetuation of Africa's partition.

For the new African political elite, Pan-Africanism as a practical policy threatened its influence over its own nation state. Practical Pan-Africanism was perceived by this elite as a challenge to their right to run their own territories. These petty jealousies became consolidated in the sixties, and the preservation of the existing political maps became of paramount concern to Africa's leaders. Any attempt to challenge Africa's colonial heritage was dismissed as unrealistic or as a recipe for chaos.

Even within Ghana, resistance to Pan-Africanist policies was considerable. Many political leaders and civil servants warned Nkrumah that his Pan-Africanist policies should not be at Ghana's expense. Within months of Ghana's independence, Nkrumah was made aware of the strength of feeling against his attempt to give Pan-Africanism a practical edge. In 1958, Nkrumah underlined his commitment to African unity by bringing the veteran Pan-Africanist, George Padmore, to Ghana. Nkrumah's intention was to make Padmore his adviser on African questions and to give him an appropriate cabinet post. It soon became clear that there was considerable opposition, even within the leadership of the CPP, to such an appointment. It was argued that a foreigner from the West Indies could not join the cabinet as it would put in question the government's national credentials. In the end Nkrumah bypassed these objections by establishing the Bureau of African Affairs, which was placed under Padmore's charge.

Despite the reservations of sections of the CPP leadership, Nkrumah pressed on with his Pan-Africanist policy. As early as April 1958, a conference was organised in Accra, which brought together the eight African governments independent at the time: Ethiopia, Liberia, Morocco, Tunisia, Libya, Egypt, Sudan and Ghana. The declaration passed by the conference emphasised the centrality of assisting the liberation struggles in Algeria and South Africa. Later in the year, in December 1958, an All-African People's Conference was held in Ghana. This was the first genuinely All-African assembly since it brought together representatives from all parts of Africa. It also brought together for the first time all the freedom movements in Africa. By the end of the fifties, Accra had emerged as the headquarters of Pan-Africanism.

Through Nkrumah's initiative, agencies like the African Affairs Secretariat and the All-African Trade Union Federation were established. At least a strong base for Pan-Africanism was established in Nkrumah's Ghana.

The focus of Nkrumah's foreign policy was the establishment of a unitary African state. Nkrumah's call for a 'Union Government for Africa' was compelling, and even those African leaders who opposed it did not dare to take a stand publicly. For a while it appeared that Nkrumah's policies were on the verge of a breakthrough. In November 1958, the formation of the Ghana–Guinea Union represented the first tentative step towards African unification. This union attracted the support of Mali in 1961. However, this was as far as matters went. In 1950, many ex-colonies became independent. Most of the new states were small, inherently unstable and relatively conservative governments. Most of the leaders of the ex-French colonies had strong allegiances to the metropolitan power and were profoundly hostile to the Pan-Africanist project. By 1961 it had become clear that the majority of the newly independent states were not prepared to countenance any practical measures towards the realisation of the Pan-Africanist ideal. The Organisation of African Unity (OAU) which was established in 1963 represented a compromise. At least an All-Africa framework for political discussion was in existence. But it was a compromise which directly contradicted the spirit of Pan-African unity. It substituted an irrelevant talking shop for the objective of an All-African government. Isolated, Nkrumah decided to suspend his campaign for a union government of Africa and sought to influence the OAU in a Pan-Africanist direction. Nkrumah hoped that events would confirm his analyses and that the membership of the OAU would be susceptible to change.

During the years 1963–6 it became painfully clear that the majority of the OAU membership was hostile to any steps towards the consolidation of African unity. In these years Africa stood helpless and divided as its sovereignty was trampled on by imperialist powers. Serious conflicts erupted between Somalia and Kenya. Army mutinies in Kenya, Tanzania and Uganda were put down with the help of British troops rather than with the assistance of fellow African states. In Zimbabwe the white minority regime of Ian Smith declared UDI and dared the rest of Africa to make a move. In Zaïre, foreign troops ran the country, ignoring the aspirations of the local population. At the second conference of the OAU in 1964, Nkrumah did some plain talking: 'Every day we delay the establishment of a Union Government of Africa, we subject ourselves to outside economic domination. And our political independence as separate states becomes more and more meaningless.' According to Nkrumah a divided Africa had made it possible for imperialism to do what it wished. On an optimistic note he continued:

> Great things are in store for us if we could but take courage in our hands and reach out towards them. How would South Africa dare to silence Nelson Mandela and his seven brave colleagues against protests of a United Africa? How would Portugal dare to think of continuing the violation of sovereignty of Angola or Mozambique or so-called 'Portuguese Guinea', if these formed part of a United Government of Africa? How could a white settler minority government in Southern Rhodesia dare to lock up Nkomo and Sithole?[6]

This vision made little impression on the conservative African leaders. As long as they retained control over their own union government it did not apparently matter what went on elsewhere in the continent. The OAU's paralysis and hostility can be seen as a testimony to Nkrumah's failure to win support from the political leadership of the new Africa. This setback, however, did not defeat Nkrumah's enthusiasm to fight on for Pan-Africanism.

The record of the Nkrumah government stands in sharp contrast to the lethargy of the OAU. The foreign policy of Ghana exuded the spirit of Pan-Africanism. In 1958 when the newly established independent state of Guinea was confronted with economic war from France, Nkrumah acted decisively. He mobilised his influence on behalf of Guinea and helped consolidate the power of the newer regime. A $10 million interest-free loan from Ghana indicated that Pan-African solidarity was state policy.

When the newly established Patrice Lumumba government of the Congo (now Zaïre) faced foreign threat, Nkrumah ushered in assistance. The battalions of Ghanaian troops and a group of engineers and doctors were promptly despatched to the Congo.

6 Ibid., p. 288.

Lumumba was a close co-thinker of Nkrumah and also a committed Pan-Africanist. Although elected as a legitimate head of state, Lumumba faced an armed revolt orchestrated by Belgium. Nkrumah understood that the stakes were high. If Lumumba fell, the cause of Pan-Africanism would be severely set back. On 8 August 1960, he warned the Ghana National Assembly:

> This is the turning point in the history of Africa. If we allow the independence of the Congo to be compromised in any way by the imperialist and capitalist forces, we shall expose the sovereignty and independence of all Africa to grave risk. The struggle of the Congo is therefore our struggle. It is incumbent on us to take our stand by our brothers in the Congo in the full knowledge that only Africa can fight for its destiny.[7]

A secret agreement signed between Nkrumah and Lumumba committed both governments to work for the establishment of a union of African states. Tragically, the agreement was never implemented. In September the Lumumba government was overthrown, and in 1961 Nkrumah's close ally was murdered. In retrospect it can be argued that the defeat of the Lumumba government represents a turning-point in the Nkrumah experiment. The defeat of Lumumba greatly undermined the strength of the Pan-Africanist forces. It heightened Ghana's and Nkrumah's sense of isolation. To make matters worse, the complicity of a number of African puppet regimes in the downfall of Lumumba indicated that unity was still an elusive dream.

For Nkrumah the rape of the Congo was a traumatic event. It forced him to re-evaluate his thinking and provided him with new insights about the nature of the African revolution. Nkrumah's popularisation of the term 'neo-colonialism' can be seen as the product of bitter experience. The tragedy of the Congo revealed the charade of independence. The old colonial powers were still able to influence events through their hand-picked African puppet regimes. Writing in 1965, Nkrumah defined neo-colonialism in the following way:

7 Ibid., p. 288.

The essence of neo-colonialism is that the state which is subject to it is, in theory, independent and has all the outward trappings of international sovereignty. In reality, its economic system and thus its political policy is directed from outside.[8]

It was this understanding of realities that led Nkrumah to realise that African unity could not be achieved without a struggle against the more subtle forms of domination and influence.

It can be argued that Lumumba's overthrow anticipated Nkrumah's own downfall. These two events showed that the pursuit of real Pan-Africanism was a dangerous business. The enemies of this goal both inside and outside Africa were too strong to make any serious headway. But a start had been made, and it can be argued that, with Nkrumah, Pan-Africanism ceased to be a dream though it was not yet a reality. More to the point, Nkrumah's programme for African unity had withstood the test of time and has a compelling relevance for today's conditions.

A Programme for Action

In January 1963, Nkrumah worked out a four-point positive programme for African unity. An examination of this programme shows that it is probably even more relevant today than when it was written. The first point of the programme advocated a common foreign policy and diplomacy for Africa. As Nkrumah argues, an Africa divided into a collection of small states can never influence international events. On the contrary, such fragmented small nations will necessarily become the objects rather than the subjects of global diplomacy. The large industrial powers could easily dominate a divided Africa. As Nkrumah wrote: 'The desirability of a common foreign policy which will enable us to speak with one voice in the councils of the world is so obvious, vital and imperative that comment is hardly necessary.'[9]

8 Ibid., pp. 147–8.
9 Ibid., p. 314.

Today, the fatal consequences of a divided Africa in the sphere of foreign affairs is all too obvious. It is Western power blocs that decide the future of Africa. Even on matters of direct concern to Africans, such as the issue of apartheid in South Africa, all the important decisions and negotiations take place in Washington, Paris or London. Africa is littered with foreign military bases, and, too often, the new states' foreign policies articulate those of their old colonial masters.

The second point of Nkrumah's programme calls for 'common continental planning for economic and industrial development in Africa'. Nkrumah observed that in natural resources Africa is rich and yet in economic terms it is poor. Only a division of labour established on a continent-wide basis could reverse this state of affairs. The profound economic crisis that faces Africa shows the importance of Nkrumah's analysis. Since Nkrumah's death, deterioration of Africa's fabric puts an all-African economic perspective firmly on the agenda.

The third point of Nkrumah's programme demands 'a common currency, a monetary zone and a central bank of issue'. Control over Africa's economy demands co-ordination of its finance. Otherwise it will be foreign banks that will dominate Africa's resources. In recent times Africa's decline has been vividly shown by its indebtedness to foreign banks. Indeed, the proportion of Africa's resources which is devoted to the payment of interest on foreign loans is so high that there is virtually nothing for productive investment. As long as it is foreign banks that control Africa's finance there can be no real economic development.

The fourth point calls for a common defence and security system with an African high command in order to ensure the stability and security of Africa. According to Nkrumah, a united military force is essential for the preservation of Africa's integrity. Today, such a military force is long overdue. It could play a vital role in assisting the liberation forces in southern Africa and thus ridding the continent of the last vestiges of direct colonialism. A coherent system of defence could also assist in the removal of foreign military bases and help African nations such as Libya which face imperialist aggression.

No doubt Nkrumah's programme could be updated and made more specific to cover issues of the day. For what is at stake is not specifics but a perspective for African liberation. Nkrumah's warnings about what would happen to a divided Africa have proved all too true. It was his merit that he understood that national independence did not constitute liberation. As he himself stated, the 'independence of Ghana is meaningless unless it is linked up with the total liberation of Africa'.[10] This is a message that will simply not go away. Ghana's own experience serves as its living proof. Nkrumah's perspectives for African unity are the distillation of vital historical lessons. It is the only road that holds out a future for the continent. A slave or a master of its destiny? It is a choice that all Africans have to make. Nkrumah's example provides them with the inspiration to do what is necessary.

10 Ibid.

Conclusion

Nkrumah for Our Times

Nkrumah did not recognise defeat. The CIA-backed army coup which overthrew his government could not destroy the man. More importantly, Nkrumah's message continued to come across loud and clear, winning thousands of new adherents to his cause across the world.

Of his exile in Guinea, Nkrumah writes in a matter-of-fact, sober way:

> On Wednesday, the 2nd of March 1966, I arrived in Conakry, Guinea, at the invitation of the President, Sékou Touré and the Guinean people, and here began what I consider to be one of the most fruitful periods of my life. For, in a secluded villa by the sea, my enforced freedom from the day to day work of the government leaves me time to study, to prepare actively for the next phase of the African revolution, when all methods of struggle, including the use of armed force, both conventional and unconventional, may be employed.[1]

That Nkrumah could refer to his exile as 'one of the most fruitful periods' of his life is itself remarkable. Most politicians would have become demoralised and have faded away under such circumstances. Nkrumah did not need the trappings of state power to maintain his influence. Through deepening his perspective for African liberation, Nkrumah was at the same time shaping the

1 Nkrumah, *Revolutionary Path*, p. 389.

future of political discourse. It was in Conakry that the present author had the good fortune to work closely and discuss seriously with the exiled leader. Nkrumah had no time for those who looked back to the glories of the past and gave vent to their self-pity. Several times he told those with him to 'look to the future so that the opportunities for change do not elude you'. For many of us, youthful associates of Nkrumah, it was difficult to grasp why he was so immune to the trauma of exile. It was almost as if Nkrumah had acted as if what he was doing in Conakry was just as important as his achievements in Ghana during the previous period.

It is only now, much later on, that it becomes evident that Nkrumah was right. Nkrumah was one of the first to understand that the struggle for African liberation was to be a protracted one. There would be many setbacks and defeats before victory would be in sight. Moreover, Nkrumah grasped the essentially all-African character of the process of liberation. The coup in Ghana may have deprived him of a national base but he was still able to influence the struggle in Africa.

The author remembers quite well a remark made by the late Shirley DuBois after we had spent hours with the exiled President. It was the fateful day on which Eduardo Mondlane, the Mozambican nationalist leader, was assassinated by the Portuguese by means of a parcel bomb.[2] 'Incredible! Osagyefo is incredible!', the wife of the great Pan-Africanist, W. E. B. DuBois, swore as we left Nkrumah for our hotel. 'It seems his political cells have been rejuvenated,' she opined, adding: 'The imperialists will regret forever overthrowing him.' Shirley DuBois was, of course, commenting on Nkrumah's mental state after he had subjected us to nearly five hours of lecturing on Ghanaian, African and world affairs. Indeed, Nkrumah's alertness and mental rigour in his days of exile were incredible.

During the years of exile, Nkrumah's home became a sort of unofficial headquarters for African liberation. For those of us who spent some time with him in exile, it was an unforgettable experience. Leading revolutionaries like Amilcar Cabral would arrive for consultations, and important discussions would take place late into the night. Nkrumah was single-mindedly concerned with influencing and educating the new generation of African activists. From

2 Nkrumah, in conversation with the author.

his experience in Ghana during previous decades, he had come to understand the importance of a well-educated cadre, steeled in the experience of mass struggle and totally committed to liberation.

Nor was Nkrumah above the task of educating himself. As a genuine revolutionary Nkrumah was not prepared to live on past glories. He knew that he had to keep up with the times and deepen his understanding of the problems of the African revolution. He also had the gift of critically evaluating his own experiences in Ghana and learning from his mistakes.

In his assessment of the Ghana experiment Nkrumah was able to develop further his theory of change and his political strategy. In his study of the African condition, he became sensitive to the formidable obstacles that stood in the way of change. His own downfall, coups in other parts of the continent and the consolidation of the settler colonisation in southern Africa, indicated that the attainment of real freedom was going to be more difficult than he ordinarily imagined. He was taken aback by the hostility of many African regimes to real change and became aware of the dimensions of the internal obstacles to liberation.

It was this process of assessment that pushed Nkrumah to reanalyse the situation and develop his concept of neo-colonialism. In line with this reassessment came a reorientation of tactics and strategy. Hitherto, Nkrumah had emphasised non-violence as the main method of the anti-imperialist struggle. However, with the experience of the previous decade it became manifest that non-violent forms of struggle could not seriously challenge the armed might of the colonial forces and the CIA-backed puppet regimes. In his book *Class Struggle in Africa*, a major reorientation in tactics is evident. Nkrumah writes:

> Under neo-colonialism a new form of violence is being used against the people of Africa. It takes the form of indirect political domination through the indigenous bourgeoisie and puppet governments teleguided and marionetted by neo-colonialists; direct economic exploitation through an extension of the operations of giant inter-locking corporations; and through all manner of other insidious ways such as the control of the mass communications media and ideological penetration.

In these circumstances, the need for armed struggle has

101

arisen once more. For the liberation and unification of Africa cannot be achieved by consent, by moral precept or moral conquest. It is only through resort to arms that Africa can rid herself of remaining vestiges of colonialism, and of imperialism and neo-colonialism; and a socialist society can be established in a free and united continent.[3]

This emphasis on the armed struggle is not the product of some morbid fascination with violence. It represents a recognition of a trend towards the armed suppression of the anti-imperialist struggle in Africa. The armed struggle is not a choice but a necessity under these conditions. This lesson has been learned by the liberation movements in southern Africa. Today, after the Anglo-American air strike in Libya and the armed invasions of Angola and Mozambique, Nkrumah's message acquires a profound relevance.

In his reassessment of tactics and strategy, Nkrumah developed his perspective on the achievement of Pan-African unity. He warned that the OAU was fast becoming an obstacle to African unity instead of a force for change:

> An examination of recent weeks exposes serious weaknesses within the OAU. The Organisation failed to solve the crisis in the Congo and Rhodesia: both of them test cases. . . . In fact the OAU is in danger of developing into a useful river for the confused sterile action of conflicting interests, the only difference being that in the context of one big brotherly organisation, reactionary tactics are camouflaged and applied through the negotiations.[4]

According to Nkrumah the OAU had become a face-saving device for many African governments who were hostile to the objectives of Pan-Africanism. Such governments could then use the inaction of the OAU as an excuse for their own lack of action on issues such as apartheid. From his review of the OAU, Nkrumah drew the conclusion that the struggle for African unity would not get very far through reliance on diplomacy and government-to-government

3 Ibid.
4 Ibid., p. 472.

negotiations. He proposed that in the future the struggle should be conducted through a unified command, co-ordinating progressive forces. In other words, Nkrumah saw the unity of like-minded forces as the point of departure for the liberation of Africa. In 1968 he argued for the establishment of the All-African People's Revolutionary Party (AAPRP) and the creation of an All-African People's Revolutionary Army. He noted:

> The formation of a political party linking all liberated territories and struggling parties under a common ideology will smooth the way for eventual unity, and will at the same time greatly assist the prosecution of the All-African people's war. To assist the process of its formation, an All-African Committee for Political Co-ordination (AACPC) should be established to act as a liaison between all parties which recognise the urgent necessity of conducting an organised ˙ and unified struggle against colonisation and neo-colonialism. This committee would be created at the level of the central committees of the ruling parties and struggling parties, and would consolidate their integrated political consciousness.[5]

With this shift in forces, Nkrumah attempted to revitalise Pan-Africanism by basing it firmly on mass movements. Nkrumah believed that through the unification of like-minded progressive forces drawn from across the continent, an effective liberation movement could emerge. Today, Nkrumah's call for an All-African military force has gained widespread support. It was raised, only to be rejected, at the 1986 meeting of the OAU. But with the expansionary ambitions of the Pretoria regime becoming a growing danger to Africa, it is only a matter of time before concerned Africans are forced to join in a united movement of resistance.

The development of Nkrumah's thought in his exile years provides Africa with a priceless legacy. The latter-day works complete a body of thought which is now recognised as one of the most original of this century. The achievement of Nkrumah is now widely recognised. C. L. R. James, the leading theorist of Pan-Africanism, considers that Nkrumah's contribution to African thought is so far-

---

5 Ibid., p. 486.

reaching that he sees him as one of the four greatest statesmen of the twentieth century, along with such giants as Lenin, Gandhi and Mao Tse-Tung.[6]

According to James, Nkrumah's ideas are of relevance to the whole black diaspora. James's favourable evaluation of Nkrumah is based on the man's synthesis of theory and action. For James, the Nkrumah regime in Ghana expressed the spirit of Pan-Africanism.

James remarked that 'never before in the most advanced political circles had any state declared that it is ready to abandon national sovereignty in the interest of a continent', and concluded that 'the policy of Ghana stands as a beacon light in the political development of the modern world'.[7]

According to Kwame Touré (formerly Stokely Carmichael): 'The highest political expression of Black Power is Pan-Africanism, and the highest expression of Pan-Africanism in Nkrumaism.'[8]

Malcolm X, the black American revolutionary, was equally impressed with Nkrumah. Such universal acclaim for Nkrumah among leading black thinkers serves as testimony to the man.

Nkrumah also had his share of critics. Political opponents and those jealous of his fame have accused Nkrumah of being hungry for power. Others have charged him with bribery and corruption. Those of us who knew him and his modest life-style can testify that such charges are absurd and born entirely out of malevolence. Others have argued that Nkrumah's writings were the work of others. It is not possible to confirm that he wrote every sentence of his articles and books. He was a busy man and no doubt used the services of advisers and research assistants. But there can be no doubt as to the authenticity of Nkrumah's ideas. His work shows a continuous ability to develop his analysis in line with changing conditions. Only a man possessing intellectual rigour and creativity of thought could have made the many insights that are evident throughout his work.

Like all great men, Nkrumah made more than his share of mistakes. That is the penalty that all those who make history are forced to pay. But to his credit, Nkrumah learned from his experiences and mistakes. As a result he always managed to stay ahead of his time. If

6 C. L. R. James, *Nkrumah and the Ghana Revolution*, London, Allison and Busby, p. 189.

7 Ibid., p. 163.

8 Ibid., p. 163.

anything, Nkrumah's greatest tragedy was the fact that he was so much ahead of those around him. Very few were able to follow the implications of Nkrumah's perspective. Even those who were often inspired by his vision could not, on their own, follow on the right road.

Nkrumah's legacy of thought retains its vitality precisely because it is the intellectual product of Africa's historical experience. With Nkrumah, ideas point the way to action and develop further through action. It is this dialectic between ideas and action that made Nkrumah such a sensitive tribune of the people. He captured the mood and aspirations of his people and translated them into a universal message for Africa and for black people everywhere. That is why African–Americans can so readily identify with the perspective outlined by him. Nkrumah requires not adulation but consideration. All Africans owe a debt of gratitude to his liberating vision. The best way to repay the debt is for a new generation of Africans to learn for themselves the value of study and political education. Africans need not only to share his dream, but also to share his determination to build a new Africa.

Bibliography

Below are listed the major works of Kwame Nkrumah, to which the author has appended some brief comments.

Africa Must Unite, London, William Heinemann, 1964. This is the best advocacy for African unity. Published soon after the 1963 Addis Ababa summit at which the OAU was established as a loose union without the necessary powers to tackle the problems facing the continent, the book is based on the author's conviction that 'no single part of Africa can be safe or free to develop fully and independently, while any part remains unliberated, or while Africa's vast economic resources continue to be exploited by imperialist and neocolonialist interests'. Only a united government of all African countries, the author argues, can lead to the economic liberation of the continent.

Autobiography of Kwame Nkrumah, London, William Heinemann, 1957. First printed in paperback in 1959, it was reprinted in 1960, 1961, 1965 and 1973. It is the moving, human story of Kwame Nkrumah's chronicle from childhood to his dynamic leadership of the liberation struggle and the attainment of Ghana's independence in 1957. In fact, it is the story of Ghana, and an incisive insight into the politics of the Gold Coast and how independence was won.

Axioms, London, Panaf Books, 1967. A pocket-sized book containing short key extracts from the writings and speeches of the foremost exponent of African liberation, unity and socialism. It is a book of quotable quotes from the author.

Challenge of the Congo, London, Panaf Books, 1967. A detailed case study of foreign pressures on an independent state. As one of the principal actors in the Congo crisis of 1960–4, Nkrumah throws new light on the events that rocked the Congo a few weeks after it attained independence on 30 June 1960, covering Katanga's secession, the failure of the UN peace-keeping operation, the murder of Congolese Premier, Patrice Lumumba, foreign military intervention at Stanleyville, and the seizure of power by Mobutu. A most valuable and unusual feature is the publication of contemporary diplomatic records on which future historical analysis can be based.

Class Struggle in Africa, London, Panaf Books, 1970. Recent African history has exposed the close links between the interests of imperialism and neo-colonialism and the African bourgeoisie. This book reveals the nature and extent of the class struggle in Africa, and sets it in the broad context of the African revolution and the world socialist revolution.

Consciencism, London, William Heinemann, 1964. In this book Nkrumah offers an ideology for the success of the African Revolution. He outlines his philosophical beliefs relating them to the special problems of Africa and states his case for scientific socialism as the essential and logical development from Africa's socio-political heritage.

Dark Days in Ghana, London, Panaf Books, 1968. In exile in Conakry after the coup that toppled his government on 24 February 1966, Kwame Nkrumah examines the coup and its implications for Ghana and the African liberation struggle in its entirety. The book successfully shows the alliance between local reactionary elements and the interests of imperialists and neo-colonialists in preventing the implementation of socialist policies in one African country and the obstacles all such countries are likely to face for their progressive stance.

Handbook of Revolutionary Warfare, London, Panaf Books, 1968. This book provides a practical guide for the armed phase of the African liberation struggle. When it was written Nkrumah lived so close to Guinea-Bissau, then undergoing guerrilla warfare for its freedom, that he was able to study at close hand the dynamics of the armed struggle. In clear and precise terms he sets down the structure for an all-African political and military organisation for the final victory of the African people and the achievement of total liberation of all Africa and a united government for the continent. He exposes both the external and internal forces who are insidiously thwarting the aspirations of the African people.

I Speak of Freedom, London, William Heinemann, 1961. A selection from the speeches of Kwame Nkrumah up to 1960, linked by narrative. The main theme is Ghana's independence and post-independence reconstruction – political freedom preparing the way for a socialist programme of economic and social development. It also shows how Ghana's independence (and, for that matter, the independence of any other African state) is linked to the total liberation of the continent and its eventual unification.

Neo-Colonialism: the Last Stage of Imperialism, London, Panaf Books, 1965. First published in 1965 by Nelson, it caused such an uproar in the US State Department that a sharp note of protest was sent to Kwame Nkrumah and $35 million of American 'aid' to Ghana was promptly cancelled by the Johnson administration. It exposes the workings of international monopoly capitalism in Africa, and shows how the stranglehold of foreign monopolistic complexes perpetuates the paradox of Africa: poverty in the midst of plenty. Political freedom without economic independence is meaningless. The solution, according to the author, lies in unification and an All-African Union government.

Revolutionary Path, London, Panaf Books, 1973. This book was compiled during the last two years of the author's life. It was begun in response to many requests for a single volume which would contain key documents, some of them previously unpublished, relating to the devel-

opment and consistency of Kwame Nkrumah's political thought, and
which would at the same time illustrate landmarks in his career as a
leading theorist and activist of the world socialist struggle. Among the
documents included in Parts 1 and 2 are editorials from the *Accra
Evening News*, 'What I Mean by Positive Action', the 'Motion of Destiny',
the 'Dawn Broadcast', and the full text of other important speeches and
broadcasts. Part 3 contains key sections from books and pamphlets
written in Conakry between 1966 and 1971. Introductory sections to
each document provide further insight into the author's political thinking.

Rhodesia File, Panaf Books, 1976. The book contains key documents
from the file on Rhodesia which Kwame Nkrumah opened shortly after
the unilateral declaration of independence by the settler regime on 11
November 1965. They relate mainly to the crucial years 1964-6. The
letters and other documents, published for the first time, show the thinking of Nkrumah on the whole question of minority regimes in Africa·
within the context of the total liberation of southern Africa. A connecting
narrative and chronology of main events in the history of Rhodesia from
1887 have been added by the publishers to provide background material
and continuity.

The Struggle Continues, London, Panaf Books, 1973. A collection of
six pamphlets written by Nkrumah both during the period of struggle for
Ghana's independence and when he was in exile, this book illustrates the
indomitable spirit of Kwame Nkrumah, the symbol of fighting Africa.
The first pamphlet, 'What I Mean by Positive Action', was written in
1949 when the campaign for the independence of Ghana was at its
height. The other five pamphlets were all written between 1966 and
1968 in Conakry, where the author examined various aspects of the
revolutionary struggle.

Towards Colonial Freedom, London, William Heinemann, 1973. This
little classic, completed in 1945 and first published in 1962 by Heinemann, is the first book written by Nkrumah. The author diagnoses the ills
of colonialism and, most important of all, prescribes a way out of colonial
bondage. In Nkrumah's words: 'Most of the points I made have been
borne out to the letter, and confirmed by subsequent events in Africa and
Asia.'

Voice from Conakry, London, Panaf Books, 1967. Broadcasts to the
people of Ghana made in Conakry by Kwame Nkrumah in 1966 on
Radio Guinea's 'Voice of the Revolution'. Their purpose was, first, to
expose the true nature of the *coup d'état* of 24 February 1966 that overthrew Nkrumah; and, second, to encourage popular resistance.

This Bibliography has been prepared with the help of Panaf Books.

Index